TELEGRAPH PEOP

Telegraph People

Behind the scenes in the heyday of a city's
multi-edition evening newspaper

Mirrorpix

John Lamb

This edition published 2019 by:
Takahe Publishing Ltd.
Registered Office:
77 Earlsdon Street, Coventry CV5 6EL

ISBN 978-1-908837-12-7

TAKAHE PUBLISHING LTD.

2019

For

Ann, Joanne, James, Maria

and

Annabel, Olivia and Eva

Acknowledgements

There are many people to thank for helping and encouraging me to write this book. They include:

Chris Arnot, Rob Beaufoy, Jerry Blackett, Bob Cole, Steve Dyson, Dan Harrison, Liz Holmes, Ian Hume, Roger Monkman, Peter Prestidge, Annette Witheridge...thanks for your patience

Also for their encyclopaedic knowledge of their life-long passion, Coventry City Football Club (the Sky Blues):

Billy Boyd, Rich Tootall Snr, Rich Tootall Jnr

...and, of course, I could not have done this without the help, experience and expertise of publisher Steve Hodder.

Cover design: Mark Scarborough, creative director, Primal Pop Ltd, Halesowen

Thanks to all of you

Every effort has been made to trace and give proper credit for all of the pictures and illustrations in Telegraph People. Please contact the publisher if you can identify any un-credited material.

CONTENTS

Welcome

From a life-long newspaperman

The *Coventry Telegraph's* former headquarters in Corporation Street, their home for nearly 60 years, are to become a hotel. I was there on the day they moved in and that prompted me to write this book. It's not about the bricks and mortar but the people who worked in it.

Those *Telegraph* people became valued colleagues as we shared the daily excitement and dramas of publishing a multi-edition evening paper, changing pages on the day as the news broke.

The newspaper was loved (sometimes hated) by what were an estimated 350,000 daily readers. And its now-defunct *PINK* Saturday night sports stablemate is still missed.

Sadly, most former regional evening newspapers today are produced overnight like the national morning papers, so can't be updated as the news develops during the day.

I was privileged to be a journalist at a time when newspapers were in their pomp and I witnessed the final days of Fleet Street, once the epicentre of the newspaper world. How many jobs give you the opportunity to indulge your passions and interests – and get paid for it? Yes, we were paid, albeit not very much.

My three spells at the *Telegraph* – between 1960 and 1982 – were broken with jobs on the *Birmingham Mail*, the *London Evening News*, the *Daily Mirror*, the *News of the World*, the *Sun*, the *London Evening Standard* and the *Birmingham Post*.

I really didn't have itchy feet but I took action in the light of circumstances, opportunities and disappointments as they came my way.

Telegraph People

Initially, the *Telegraph* wouldn't give me a job because I had left Barkers Butts School in Coventry only with a certificate for swimming a length at breaststroke and four London College of Music certificates for piano playing and music theory.

None of these successes had anything to do with the efforts of the school which, as a secondary modern, regarded most of their pupils as failures because they had not passed the 11+. The brainy kids who did pass went to the schools of King Henry VIII or Bablake in Coventry. My mum and dad, Maud and George, paid for the piano lessons.

When I told the careers master I wanted to be a musician or an architect he guffawed. He recovered enough to give me a note of introduction to become an apprentice at an electrical firm in the city.

Well I never made it as an electrician but landed three jobs on the *Telegraph* – copy boy, deputy sports editor and then No 2 to the editor over a span of 22 years.

The *Telegraph* now operates from offices on the opposite side of the ring road from Corporation Street in the canal basin in Leicester Row.

Back at Corporation Street, I always felt a frisson of excitement going through those heavy doors on the corner of the building. Each was embellished with a brass centrepiece with "*Coventry Evening Telegraph*" etched on it.

As you bounded up the stairs to the first floor, you knew you were going to join 100 colleagues who took great pride in producing a cracking newspaper, breaking news during the course of the day. Memories of the noises, the rows, the distinctive smells of highly industrialised processes linger even today.

And you could parcel up that all-consuming package and transfer it to the Town Wall Tavern after work. There the day's joys, disappointments, balls ups, crazy encounters, unbelievable decisions by the editor and his underlings plus yet another memo about gerunds and split infinitives would be dissected and regularly ridiculed.

Tempers would soar along with the alcohol intake. There would be impassioned interventions from union officials and heady talk about action over some trivia. But we all knew that in the morning we would be back at our desks overlooking Belgrade Square praying for that elusive world scoop.

My account is of a different age from today's digital world. Online newspapers, blogs and social media posts on the likes of Twitter, Facebook and LinkedIn were years away and the *Telegraph* was largely produced in hot metal. Sweaty editorial floors were littered with the detritus of the day's production, a far cry from today's sanitised offices.

I still envy anyone who has embarked on a career in journalism, whether in print or online, radio or television. It's a very different role today but retains for me that innate sense of working in the best job ever created.

Anyone going into journalism today cannot have made a better choice if they want a career that embodies great skills, passion and the sheer thrill of working in a high-pressure environment with like-minded colleagues.

Despite a general abhorrence of the media in some quarters, most journalists right across the spectrum of international, national and local news and sport in all its forms are dedicated to seeking out the truth, no matter how painful.

There are real dangers. In 2018, 94 journalists died in the pursuit of stories. And amid the frenetic race to get stories and pictures back to the office, there are dangers of a less life-threatening nature.

A misplaced hyphen or wrong word can result in expensive libel claims and when you consider all the pressures newspapers are under they generally put together an amazing product in a remarkably short time.

I believe journalism is the greatest career anyone could choose. It is under threat as never before and I do believe that it should be cherished to ensure the very preservation of healthy democracies.

I don't imagine print can last for much longer, with circulations plummeting and no-one seeming capable or willing to arrest the decline.

We always used to insist on a high story-count but today you're lucky if you get two stories a page in print because publishers want to push you to their websites for a fuller news digest.

Newspapers do contrast greatly in this respect. I compared two in the Midlands. One had a total of 25 stories across 34 pages. The other had 25 by the time you got to page five out of 32 news pages packed with stories. The biggest seller? The one with the high story count.

Today's regional newspapers are a shadow of what they were largely because they now print overnight and do not have enough staff, even to answer the telephone.

They also do not seem interested in getting stories. I rang one large regional newspaper and could not get through to anyone. There was an automatic system for simply cutting off all calls to the editorial department after about 10 rings. It really does beggar belief that any company in the media business would be prepared to introduce this practice.

I know there are many more ways of communicating today but a phone call does ensure an air of confidentiality where a tipster might be prepared to give you a great story. No wonder print is going down the drain but sadly digital is no substitute.

We even hear reports that the BBC and newspaper groups have been talking to the government about plans for an independent foundation to tackle what they describe as the "chronic underreporting" of local news. Getting the government involved in newspaper content is the start of a rocky road and the issues should be tackled without their intervention.

Staffing levels have been slashed and the remaining journalists have no chance of covering institutions like the law courts and councils or even Parliament adequately. At least it's encouraging that the very existence of these talks are a tacit admission by proprietors that in many cases their coverage of local news is now inadequate.

We used to establish and maintain precious contacts by meeting them, getting to know them and developing a trust that would usually lead to their becoming invaluable sources. This could only be done by personal contact and would often lead to a tip-off off about other good stories.

Today, I work on the other side of the media fence and I am usually "interviewed" by email. How can a reporter possibly build a trusted and valuable contact by operating in this way?

I shudder to think how many scandals have gone un-reported and could name at least three major stories that have never been touched by the local media largely because they are out of touch with the communities they are supposed to serve.

I spent much of my career covering sport, when newspapers in the same group would send different and competing reporters to cover soccer matches for their own titles. Today, one reporter will be expected to write for several titles, resulting in matching views and certainly no hot competition to get the stories.

No wonder readers are voting with their feet and not buying newspapers. And what about the alternative? Trying to read online reports is almost impossible because you are continually interrupted by a barrage of advertisements, promotions and surveys. Many readers simply give up but I guess the websites still count these visits to their sites as a "click" on their readership figures.

The Saturday evening *PINK* sports edition of the *Telegraph* was a classic example of how newspapers "served" their communities. Packed with reports of junior sports, it would also carry the action of the day, with up-to-the-minute match reports, classified football and racing results plus revised league tables – all within half-an-hour of the final whistle being blown.

You get the news even more instantly now but who wouldn't still prefer to read all about the match in a printed newspaper shortly afterwards? Sadly this is no more, largely because sport outgrew printed newspapers. It became pointless to produce a Saturday *PINK* if Coventry City were playing the next day or on Monday.

The fortunes of the Sky Blues used to impact enormously on the sale of the *PINK* with circulation fluctuating between 15,000 and 30,000 depending on the result.

Digital coverage has taken its place but can never match the appeal of sitting at home or in the pub or club on a Saturday night with a pint and the *PINK*.

I believe that newspaper groups are running down the attraction of printed newspapers to prop up their own beliefs that they have no future. And, by the way, it's no coincidence that digital is much cheaper.

Digi devotees will claim that they have a "reach" of millions more readers than their hot-metal predecessors. But what they don't tell you is that the "reach" is only a potential readership and in reality a mythical figure.

Actual readership numbers are minuscule – that's why advertisers still prefer printed newspapers. It's easy to muddle figures in annual reports to justify your prejudices but I have rarely spoken to an advertiser who prefers a digital platform. In fact, print media is still the most profitable element across all newspapers.

I could name many wonderful exponents of the trade of journalism still in the business today. But they could become even greater journalists if they were backed by proprietors who were prepared to support them in their pursuit of genuine news.

I still get a great kick out of meeting my former mates on the *Coventry Evening Telegraph*. One of my earliest colleagues, who I still see today, was not a journalist but the advertisement director, Bill Bennett. Editorial and advertising departments rarely mixed but we now regularly share a pint and a natter in the Royal Oak in Earlsdon, Coventry.

Another colleague dating back to my first "tour" of Corporation Street was Bob Cole, a great character who served the *Telegraph* for many years as a photographer. He was regularly on duty along with me at Coventry rugby matches at Coundon Road and he was a great all-round snapper. He was also a talented cricketer.

I have also glimpsed Bob Panther across the occasional public house. He was a fellow office boy who took the printing route for employment.

Sadly, it is at funerals of others that I bump into my very early colleagues. Many of them were at the funeral of Ken Widdows, a sports desk colleague from my second "tour". Mourners included Alan Parr, sports editor who made me his No 2, and all-rounder Mike Malyon, nephew of the late camp comedian from Nuneaton, Larry Grayson.

There was also Scotsman Jim Marshall, who became a champion horse racing tipster, and Paul Allen, a journalist despite the fact that his dad Johnny was a *Telegraph* printer.

Phil Horsfall and the now-deceased *PINK* editor Greg Oliver were also valued sport desk colleagues at a time when our efforts were greatly appreciated in the Coventry region, producing truly absorbing sports pages.

From my last "tour" as assistant editor I still see former features editor Chris Arnot, now an author of several niche books and fellow Oak habitué, along with Pete Walters, both talented feature writers.

Roger Harrabin, who was one of the juniors I tried to train on the *Telegraph* when I was assistant editor in the early Eighties, is now the BBC's environmental analyst. It is the company run by Roger's brothers, Ian and Brian, that won the contract to redevelop the Corporation Street building as the *Telegraph Hotel* and student accommodation.

Among Roger's colleagues was David Shukman, who is now science editor of BBC News. The former Etonian is one of the nicest blokes I ever met in the newspaper world.

Annette Witheridge, one of my closest colleagues from that era, went on to make a huge success in Fleet Street on the *News of the World* among other titles. She established a highly successful news agency in New York and has only recently returned to the UK.

Editor Geoff Elliott spanned all of my three *Telegraph* "tours" and he was a talented all-round journalist and leader writer who re-shaped the *Telegraph* into a respected and vibrant evening newspaper. I hope my few years as his No 2 contributed to that.

He was a contemporary of Fred Bromwich, who left the *Telegraph* to work on the *Birmingham Post and Mail*. We're still colleagues at Birmingham Press Club, the oldest in the world, where he is deputy chairman and I'm a former chairman and now vice-president.

There were many others who went on to greater things. Like Dave Brindle (Guardian), Andy Grice (Independent) and Rachel Campey (editor, *Evening Herald* in Plymouth, the *Express & Echo* in Exeter and the *Yorkshire Post*).

Jim Gallagher was also on the *Telegraph* during my time and our careers met again on the *London Evening Standard*. He then went to *Today* and moved to America as a freelance. After a spell on *Sunday World* in Ireland, he now freelances there.

It would be remiss of me not to mention Roger Monkman. We never actually worked together on the *Telegraph* but our careers crossed paths on many occasions and we ended up handling the media operations of what is now called the *Greater Birmingham Chambers of Commerce*, where I am to this day director of press and PR.

Roger, like me, still can't let go of this marvellous trade and toils as editor of the *Balsall Bugle*, a community publication based in Balsall

Common, near Coventry. At least that organ is thriving and giving valuable coverage to its region.

Many other former *Telegraph* colleagues are around today and I hope they share the many fond memories I have of working in Corporation Street. Sadly others are now departed but memories of them linger.

I never worked with probably the *Telegraph's* most famous son, Jeremy Vine, star of radio and television. From everything I have read about him, he still seems to retain the same sort of pride and passion we all experienced working at the *Telegraph.*

We were privileged to share the great excitement of producing a multi-edition newspaper in a vibrant city printing around 120,000 newspapers six nights a week. The *Coventry Evening Telegraph* was the main source of the news and sport for the people of Coventry and the surrounding towns in those pre-digital days.

The ambition every day was to produce a newspaper that had a balance of international, national and local news and sport. And we managed that pretty well.

One day the main story might be local like the sacking of the Sky Blues' manager or a City Council scandal. On another day it could be the assassination of President Kennedy or the engagement of Prince Charles and Princess Di.

You wanted every major story to happen at a time when you could break the news.

This was the great challenge every day – to try to get that balance right. We *Telegraph* People worked hard to create a newspaper that did just that for those 350,000 readers every day and night.

We also played hard, as you will discover when you read on.

John Lamb, 2019

Beginning of the end

Work starts on the Coventry Evening Telegraph building on the corner of Corporation Street and Upper Well Street, converting it into the Telegraph Hotel.

CHAPTER 1

Dear Lamb...I knew my place

It was a sunny Sunday morning in the summer of 1960. The roads were quiet as I walked briskly from my parents' home into the city centre past some familiar landmarks like the Radford Club, the nearby Radford Rec (a nickname bestowed on me by friends in future years), the huge Grapes Pub, a testimony to days when hostelries like this were the centre of the community.

It had spacious-looking living quarters above for the landlord and landlady and the public rooms were large and comfortable. There was even a smoking room with a large sign on the door saying MEN ONLY. Why it was labelled a smoking room when you could smoke in all of its rooms, I don't know.

A maroon No 2 Coventry Corporation bus passed me along with a Ford Popular, which lived up to its name in those days, and as I neared the Corporation Street offices of the *Coventry Evening Telegraph*, an MG Midget whizzed past. The driver, I later learned, was also heading for the *Telegraph*.

My new employers were the *Telegraph* and they had asked me to go in early on that weekend to help their move into new offices in Corporation Street.

I had taken a job at the *Telegraph* after intending to become an apprentice electrician at a firm next to a rat-infested canal in Stoney Stanton Road, Coventry.

One night at Hill Farm Youth Club in Radford not far from my home, I was attending an art class run by a guy called Brian, who worked as an advertisement rep on the *Telegraph*.

He told me there was a vacancy for a copy boy in the sub-editors' department at the *Telegraph*. I have no idea what drove me but I applied for the job and got it, much to the concern of my dad.

I do remember, however, massively enjoying Pathe News whenever I went to the cinema, usually the Savoy on the Radford Road. That may have sewn the seeds for what developed later.

When I attended the interview at the *Telegraph's* temporary offices in Quinton Road, in the Cheylesmore district of the city, I got on well with Reg Denny, the assistant editor, and felt empathy with the atmosphere at the newspaper.

I received a type-written letter dated March 16, 1960, from Reg. I never learned why he was called Reg because he signed the letter F.A. Denny. But, then again, my first name is officially David but I have always been called John. He wrote formally offering me the job saying:

Dear Lamb

With reference to your visit to this office yesterday, I now have pleasure in offering you the position of office boy in our sub-editors' department. The starting wage will be £3.10s.0d. per week.

I would like you to start on Monday, March 28th and to report to Mr. H.Reader, Chief sub-editor, at 9 a.m. This will enable you to give a week's notice to your present employers.

Please let me have a note of your acceptance by return of post.

With best wishes and hoping you will be happy with us.

Yours sincerely,

F.A. Denny

ASSISTANT EDITOR

"Dear Lamb". You knew your place in those days...but it marked the start of a career in newspapers and publishing that is still going on today.

The reason for working on a Sunday, they told me, was that they were starting to move into their new offices and printing plant in Corporation Street in the heart of the city and could not do so during the hustle and bustle of a normal working day.

Reports have suggested that the *Telegraph* moved into Corporation Street on November 21, 1957, but that was when Lord Iliffe laid the foundation stone. It was nearly three years later before the building and the installation of the presses was completed.

I had started work a few months earlier in Quinton Road. They had relocated there after their city centre location had been damaged in the same blitz of German bombs which destroyed the city's famous cathedral and my mum and dad’s house.

But the *Telegraph* missed only one day of publishing – November 15, 1940 – and managed to carry on before moving to Quinton Road, a ramshackle collection of buildings with corrugated iron roofs near Coventry Station skirting the main Coventry to Birmingham rail line.

These offices were clearly not designed for newspaper production but I was proud to have been taken on as the copy boy in the sub-editors' department.

On my first day, I flattened the diminutive chief sub-editor Harry Reader when he pulled open the other side of the door through which I was rushing with some late copy for the next edition. Not a good start, I thought, as I lifted the bloodied Harry, replete in a three-piece suit, onto a spare chair.

The place was full of characters who I immediately warmed to. There was a sub-editor, Syd Fairlie, who tri-cycled into the office every morning from his Leamington home. To freshen up he would bathe naked in the large communal washing facilities designed for groups of printers with inky hands.

Harold Chard was Harry's deputy, assisted by the grumpy Reg Best. The sub-editors also included John Bray, who became features editor, and George Tremlett, who went on to write paperbacks on pop stars, including David Bowie.

He became a member of the now-defunct Greater London Council, where he represented Twickenham as a Conservative. I also got to know the sports guys well and would work more closely with them in the years to come.

One of my duties was to race into the city centre to collect copy from the court and council reporters and rush it back to the office. I was so proud to be trusted with such an important role that I stuck a *Telegraph* letterhead on the inside of my wallet so that I could show my 'calling credentials' as I entered the portals of either the council or courts.

I was also charged with making 12 cups of tea on the hour, every hour. Not forgetting that Barrie Clarke took eight (yes!) spoons of sugar in his black tea. I learned many years later that his teeth did, indeed, turn black and drop out.

In those days telephones were rare, certainly in my little world. We didn't have one at home and I had never used such a device. So when the phone rang on the desk of the assistant editor, Reg Denny, in his office partitioned with large glass windows overlooking the main office, I was reluctant to rush into action.

"Answer the fucking phone," someone shouted at me. I walked slowly into Reg's office hoping the call would end. I was in a cold sweat as I picked up the black, Bakelite phone and after whispering "hello" I had no recollection of what was said. It might have been a world scoop and I regret to this day that I didn't have the nous to find out.

Many years later I had Reg's job but did not have the luxury he enjoyed in employing someone like me to look after some of his many chores. One of them was for me to count the words in readers' letters to the editor. They were mostly hand-written. He could then assess how much space they would take when turned into type. This was called "casting off".

One of my other roles was to collect proofs of the stories that had been held over for lack of space from the previous day's paper. They would either be rescued for the next day or "killed", a common word in newspaper practice which left no doubt about the fate of the story.

When first asked to fetch them, I couldn't catch what Harry called them. It sounded like a German word to me and when I presented myself to the head printer's desk, I mumbled something about collecting the "overbermfuhrer" proofs. The head printer knew what I meant immediately. "You mean the overmatter proofs," he said.

Around this time I realised working for a newspaper was what I wanted to do. I really didn't know or mind in which role but for some reason I felt I had an aptitude for journalism and I had certainly developed a buzz of excitement about producing a daily newspaper, no matter how lowly my role.

My big problem was that I didn't have a relevant qualification to my name. So I decided I needed to start studying and embarked on correspondence courses for O-levels in English and British Constitution.

I had quickly learned that the big earners in newspapers at this time were the printers, who also held most of the power. They could easily stop the newspaper if any of their demarcation lines were crossed.

My counterpart in the inkies' department was an affable character called Bob Panther and he indeed went on to become a printer. His role was pretty much guaranteed because Bob's 6ft 6in frame made him a certainty as a mean fast bowler in the *Telegraph* cricket team.

So he joined the printers, where nepotism (although I don't think so in Bob's case) was rife. The well-paid jobs were much sought-after and were handed down from father to son, from uncle to nephew, from aunt to niece.

The move to a newly-built office bespoke for a newspaper and printing works in Corporation Street was an exciting prospect to which we all looked forward.

All lit up for Christmas

Placing a Christmas tree on the corner balcony of the Evening Telegraph building became a tradition.

Dear Lamb…

The letter of confirmation appointing John Lamb to the role of office boy (copy boy) in the sub-editor's department at £3 10s 0d a week.

The Coventry
Evening Telegraph
COVENTRY NEWSPAPERS LIMITED

LONDON OFFICE
80 FLEET STREET E.C.4
TELEPHONE: FLEET 2695

QUINTON ROAD
COVENTRY
TELEPHONE: 25588 COVENTRY
TELEGRAMS: TELEDV, COVENTRY

16th March, 1960.

John Lamb,
106, Cheveral Avenue,
Radford,
Coventry.

Dear Lamb,

With reference to your visit to this office yesterday, I now have pleasure in offering you the position of office boy in our sub-editors' department. The starting wage will be £3.10s.0d. per week.

I would like you to start on Monday, March 28th and to report to Mr. H. Reader, Chief Sub-editor, at 9 a.m. This will enable you to give a week's notice to your present employers.

Please let me have a note of your acceptance by return of post.

With best wishes and hoping you will be happy with us,

Yours sincerely,

F.A.Denny
ASSISTANT EDITOR

Stark reality - Quinton Road

Looking like one of Stalin's forced labour camps, the Coventry Evening Telegraph's headquarters in Quinton Road. They moved to their city centre headquarters in Corporation Street in 1960 and now those offices are to be converted into a hotel. The Quinton Road headquarters were alongside the main Coventry to Birmingham rail line.

Centre of operations - 1960-style

Nerve-centre of the Coventry Evening Telegraph...1960-style. John Lamb is framed in the window behind the main news sub-editors' T-shaped table, poised for action.

The sub-editors are (left to right): Harold Chard, deputy chief sub (chief sub Harry Reader must have been on day off); grumpy Reg Best; Syd Fairlie, the naked tri-cyclist; John Bray (back of head); Tom Cartwright; unknown; George Tremlett. Standing in the background on the right is Reg Denny, assistant editor, whose job John eventually had. Seated is Ken Burgess, who was probably in charge of features.

This was the sub-editors' room at the Telegraph's temporary building in Quinton Road, their location after the original city centre headquarters were damaged by bombing during the Second World War.

Their new city centre home was in Corporation Street. In the foreground is the sports desk, whose absent occupants may well have been in the pub.

Taking shape

The new headquarters take shape in Corporation in the late 1950s. The outline of the final shape of the building, framed by huge girders, can be clearly seen as cars typical of the day drive past.

Bob Cole

CHAPTER 2

Wind-driven copy but don't touch the type!

My first task on that Sunday morning was to carry new furniture into the sub-editors' department on the first floor overlooking Belgrade Square and the theatre on the other side. The contrast to Quinton Road could not have been greater. The large room was carpeted and there were cloakrooms with sliding doors along one wall.

At one end there was a "serving" hatch to what was called the Creed Room. The Creed housed the machines that received stories and pictures from around the country and, indeed, the world.

These were supplied by a splendid organisation called the Press Association, which still thrives today supplying national and most large regional newspapers with news and sport from home and abroad.

The Creed was named after Frederick George Creed (October 6, 1871 - December 11, 1957), a Canadian who spent most of his adult life in Britain. He worked in telecommunications and developed the teleprinter, which enjoyed its greatest fame when used by BBC Television to screen soccer results as they came in.

The large room housed only sub-editors. It was some time before huge open plan editorial floors became fashionable in Coventry.

At the top of the room, on the other side of the Creed Room's hatch, was the news sub-editors' table. It was arranged in a "T" shape, with the chiefs across the top and the "Indians" ranged down each side of the longer stem.

Tracing down the room, the features desk was next, also arranged in a similar "T" shape but much smaller, as was the sports desk at the other end, nearest the composing room where the newspaper was put together in hot metal.

But the biggest advance for me was a labyrinth of pipes about four inches in diameter. Air was sucked pneumatically through them and I would wrap the news copy into a clear plastic tube, seal it with a clip, open the air trap and push it up the tube which would carry it swiftly to the printers, thus saving chief sub-editor Harry Reader from further serious injury.

These tubes were similar to those used in department stores for carrying cash and receipts to and from the finance department. I also used to receive copy from the reporters' room by the same technology.

The system was not, for some reason, linked to the Creed Room and a small shelf underneath the hatch would rapidly fill with copy, kept in place by a large lump of metal out of which the type was made. I would frequently have to react to shouts of "Creed copy, for fuck's sake." At which point I would leap from my desk to gather and sort the news and sport from all around the world.

I often wondered why many orders made to me were accompanied by the F-word but came to realise bad language was commonplace in newspaper offices. It is said that swearing demonstrates a lack of articulacy, not a favourable trait for journalists, I suppose.

Usually, if there was a sensational story like man's landing on the moon or Fidel Castro coming to power after the revolution in Cuba, one of the guys in the Creed room would poke his head out of the hatch and shout: "News flash..."

Deadlines were paramount, of course, because at that time the *Telegraph*, circulation around 120,000 a day, published seven editions every day. They started with the Lunch Edition (off the stone at 11am, the stone being the metal bench on which the pages were made up), the Late City (2pm), the City Final (3.10) and the Night Final (4.55) plus three district editions for Leamington and Stratford, Nuneaton and Bedworth and Rugby.

The first and last editions were popular with people betting on horse racing. The very latest cards (later than the dailies) would be published in the Lunch Edition and the Night Final would carry most of the results, with the latest in the Late News column (known as 'the box') across the bottom of the back page. Readers would queue outside the office for the Night Final.

The district editions would have different front pages of local news, sometimes reduced to one or two stories on a slow day. However, if there was a major national or international story breaking that would take over most of the front page. The sports desk guys would always endeavour to get a local story on the back page of the district editions. The late news was also used for doing exactly what it was supposed to do.

But on one occasion it was used to correct an error in a recipe in the "women's supplement" called Eve. The page had been broken up so it couldn't be corrected without setting all the material in metal again.

The recipe in the page advised: "The chocolate cake requires the following ingredients: 6oz unsalted butter; 6oz caster sugar; 2 large eggs; 3oz plain chocolate; 3lb cocoa; 2 teasp baking powder; 4 fluid oz milk; 5oz plain flour; 1 teasp vanilla essence".

Three pounds of cocoa was obviously a little over the top so the features sub-editors decided to use the Late News column for the correction. It advised the readers that the "recipe in Page 8 of today's Eve should read 3oz of cocoa and not 3lb". Wrong again!

So a second correction was made advising that 3lb of cocoa should read three tablespoons. By the final edition we got it right. We never had any feedback from readers who tried to make the cake using 3lb of cocoa. But do feel free to try the recipe, being careful to convert old money ounces and pounds into metric. It sounds delicious.

One of the main rules you had to learn in newspapers was that the actual type set in metal was sacrosanct. Only members of the correct print unions were allowed to touch it and if a journalist strayed it could provoke a strike by the inkies. They would immediately go into an emergency meeting to discuss the issue, resulting in delays.

In fairness, this happened rarely on the *Telegraph* but the threat was always there throughout the industry and particularly in Fleet Street. There was some logic in these demarcation rules because if everyone was allowed to carry the type, chaos may have prevailed.

So the print unions ruled the roost but would get their comeuppance when Eddie Sha launched the digitally-produced *Today* in London in 1986. It was short-lived but sparked the revolution which saw Rupert Murdoch secretly create a digital production centre at Wapping for the *Sun*, *News of the World* and the *Sunday Times*. The inkies only found out when they turned up at Bouverie Street, off Fleet Street, to be greeted by locked doors. The resulting picket-line violence at Wapping is now history and the print unions have little or no power in newspapers.

A new beginning...

...the sub-editors' room at the new Corporation Street headquarters.

This picture was taken shortly after the building was occupied in the summer of 1960.

The new office marked a sea-change in John Lamb's life. He no longer had to run the copy into the composing room. It was carried there in plastic tubes through an air-pressured labyrinth of pipes in the picture.

At the top of the room is the hatch-door with a shelf underneath on which national and international news and pictures were placed from the Creed room next door.

The news sub-editors are immediately in front of it with the features desk next and the sports desk in the foreground. It was on the features desk that one evening a young sub-editor and his reporter girlfriend had meaningful discussions after a few attitude adjusters in the club on the floor above.

The 'tele-ad girls'

The Evening Telegraph was at the cutting edge of many innovations, especially the introduction of same-day colour pictures. This picture is another example of progress, giving readers the opportunity to place their advertisements by telephone. This considerably reduced the number of people queuing in the office which fronted Corporation Street. They were able to call in and dictate their ads to the "tele-ad girls".

Mirrorpix

CHAPTER 3

Fire! And a day of humiliation

Although my role was as copy boy in the sub-editors' department, my responsibilities were much more wide-ranging. The man who really ran the newspaper in the Sixties was Donald Beese, who took most of the duties that would normally be undertaken by the editor. At that time the editor was John Harrison, a very upright pillar of society who would not expect to get involved in the sordid business of producing a newspaper. I always felt his role was more ambassadorial than editorial.

So the brash Donald took control and ruled his empire from a small office on the "management" corridor. He always wore a dark suit and waistcoat, which during the course of the day would become covered in cigarette ash.

He was a heavy smoker and often set his waste paper basket alight. In which case he would dial my telephone number and shout "Fire!"

I had been briefed to always keep a jug of water on my desk. So I would snatch it up and sprint to the Beese office to douse the flames. I could never really understand why he didn't keep the water in his office but that was not the sort of question you asked Mr Beese, as I was required to call him.

Later, when I could understand these things, I learned that Mr Beese, like most of the upper echelon of the *Telegraph* staff, was a strong Freemason. Everyone suspected this but it was never talked about openly.

There was an atmosphere of fear in the air, proved on one of my early days. It was my duty to distribute morning newspapers to the editor and his various underlings.

Very few people had arrived by this hour – except Harry, whose early arrivals were said to be because he had a very unhappy home life. One morning I entered the editor's office, next to the corner balcony and overlooking Corporation Street, to be confronted by the chief reporter, John Poole, backing out on his hands and knees brushing the carpet as he progressed.

"Don't you mention a fucking word of this," he demanded. I realised that he had sneaked into the editor's office to have an early morning look at any interesting papers on the desk. Of course, the carpet was new and he left footprints in the pile so John, who was tall and had exceptionally large feet, would have been rumbled and he was brushing the carpet smooth. I kept it secret until now.

A day of total embarrassment and humiliation also awaited me. One of my other duties was to collect the proofs of the pages prepared early for the next day's editions. They had to be checked by the writers and the sub-editors.

Once a week, I was required to collect the theatre page proof written by Keith Whetstone under the pseudonym NKW (I think Neil was his first name but he went by Keith).

In order for the ink to take on the paper, the page had to be damp and was sometimes quite wet. When I took the page into the reporters'/writers' room, Keith complained that the paper was too wet for him to write on.

So he told me to stand on the roof in the wind until it was dry enough, causing much laughter and guffawing from his colleagues. When I protested that I had other things to do, he said there was nothing more important and that he would complain to the editor if I didn't do as I was told.

Extremely humiliated, I did as I was bid, but outside the office in Corporation Street not on the roof. Goodness knows what passersby thought I was doing. I never forgot what Keith did to me, especially when he became my editor some years later.

During my time in Corporation Street, I experienced another important character-building lesson. Word had reached me that one of the girls in the advertisement department fancied me.

I was advised by one of the more mature ladies to call Susan on her internal phone number. She was a lovely young lady and had certainly caught my eye.

But I still lacked that confidence with telephones and, anyway, I couldn't find one private enough to make the call. The prospect of having to speak to her from my desk phone filled me with the dread that everyone in the office would hear my every word.

So I did nothing. Then I had a brainwave. I went out to a public telephone box and managed to call the *Telegraph*. I don't think Susan received a lot of calls from outside and when mine was answered and I asked for her, the telephonist said: "Is that you, John?" I slammed the phone down and fled back to the office. But in the end, Susan rang me and she sounded very confident on the telephone, to my shame. I managed to mumble enough to arrange to meet her outside the Empire cinema one night.

She looked gorgeous in a short tartan skirt with a matching scarf. I don't remember what film we saw because throughout I was pre-occupied with trying to put my arm around Susan but succeeded only in getting cramp.

We parted perfectly amicably but I couldn't pluck up the courage to give her a peck on the cheek lest it was not wanted. I have since thought that she must of thought me a complete wimp. I have to report that we never met again, so I guess she voted with her feet.

One day my dad turned up at the office unannounced, asking to see Mr Denny. I found out when Reg came in to ask why my father was here. I didn't know but Reg was gracious enough to see him. My dad, who I think was disappointed that I had not started an apprenticeship, wanted to know what my prospects were.

Reg assured him that they were perfectly happy with me but he couldn't expect me to progress much further without qualifications. It was at this point that the penny dropped and I started a correspondence course in English and British Constitution O-levels.

The course was put together by Wolsey Hall in Oxford and some years later I entered their name in the education section of my CV. Wolsey Hall, Oxford, sounded impressive and I doubt anyone realised it wasn't part of Oxford University.

My dad would be pleased when another cathartic moment arrived. I was advised to apply for a job in the sports room. This was where a group of non-journalists phoned the horse racing results and other late news to the district offices of the *Telegraph*.

The staff in the far reaches – well Nuneaton, Bedworth, Rugby, Leamington and Stratford – would set our words into type on what was called a Bush machine and then print them in the late news column, which had been left blank in the papers delivered from HQ.

Anyway, this seemed a good step towards achieving my ambition of becoming a reporter and re-doubled my efforts to get educated.

So I took the sports room job. It was housed in an office on the other side of the corridor from the subs that was also occupied by the copytakers, who would type stories dictated by reporters on a telephone out on the job.

A lady, who, of course, was the wife of one of the printers, ran the department and my other colleague who liked to be called The Rock because he fancied himself as a hard-man. I'm not sure why because I had never met anyone so easy-going.

It turned out to be a fortuitous move for me. One of the regular visitors to this room was a character called Charlie Porter, who edited the *Kenilworth Weekly News,* probably the smallest newspaper in the country.

He wrote the cycling column for the *Telegraph* and its Saturday *PINK* sporting edition as a freelance and was looking for help in his proper job.

The Courier Press group owned the Kenilworth paper, which had a healthy circulation of about 4,000 in a town of around 20,000. Its stable included the *Leamington Courier* and the *Warwick Advertiser.*

Urged on by the copytakers, who knew Chas well because he often filed stories, I mentioned to him that I would like to apply for the vacancy. He took my address and at my parents' home I received a letter, written on a typewriter with big, bold letters, inviting me to "pop up for a chinwag some time".

This I did at his home in Coventry next to a bakery in the Chapelfields district of the city. I walked the three miles from home (something I subsequently did nearly every day for the next five years) for that chinwag.

He seemed to take to me because I "wasn't stuffed up with certificates" unlike a guy he had just sacked. He described him as "a Young Conservative who was useless". So I came to succeed this guy, much to the delight of my father George, a life-long Labour supporter.

And so my first stint at the *Telegraph* offices in Corporation Street came to an end – to be picked up again a few years later.

Scene of the damp proof incident

The reporters' room in the days before open-plan and the scene of a humiliating incident for John Lamb. It was here that he was embarrassed over a damp page proof by Keith Whetstone (centre foreground).

On the right is chief reporter John Poole, taking a phone call but no doubt thinking of enjoying a few lunch time pints of Guinness in a pub just over the road in one of Coventry precincts.

It was John Poole who was discovered by Lamb edging out of the editor's office on his hands and knees early one morning (see page 30).

Standing looking through a file of back numbers, which Lamb had to keep up to date, is Ernie Newbold, a very safe and steady journalist of the old school.

Future editor Keith Whetstone, who as theatre critic wrote under the pseudonym NKW, is the in centre foreground alongside Muriel Tibbs, who wrote the woman's pages.

Immediately behind them is John Cross (left), the future deputy editor, and Bill Price, who became Labour MP for Rugby between 1966 and 1979.

There is an unidentified group of reporters immediately behind them but at the top of the room is football writer Derek Henderson with David Irvine, the rugby reporter, on the phone.

The person on the right is Mike Dale, who went on to work for many years at Coventry News Service

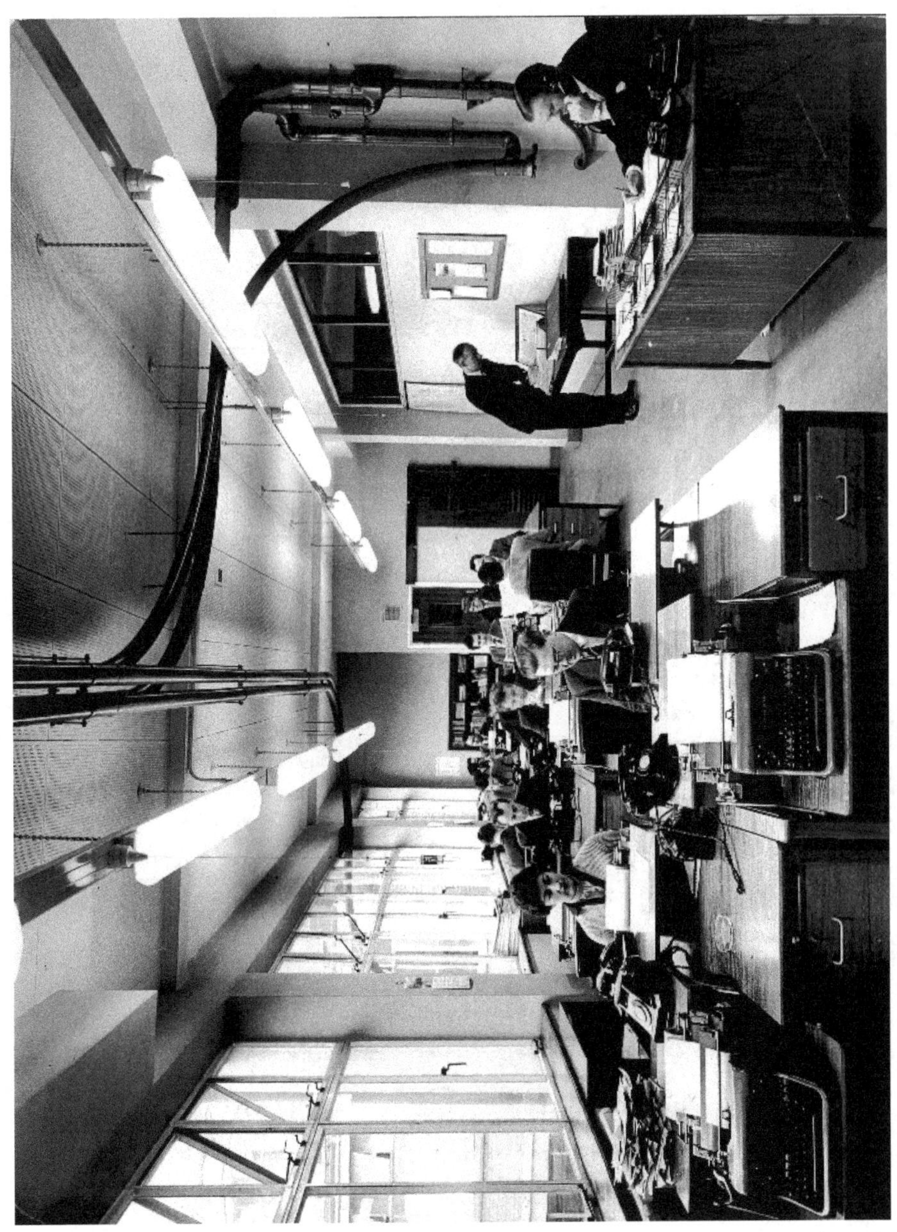

Mirrorpix

A journalist at last...

New Year's Day, 1962. A great start to the year as Lamb receives confirmation that editor Charlie Porter is prepared to give him a chance as a reporter on the Kenilworth Weekly News.

THE KENILWORTH WEEKLY NEWS

2, PRIORY ROAD, KENILWORTH, WARWICKSHIRE — Telephone 870

DIRECTORS:
J. H. WALKLEY
E. A. MARTIN

EDITOR: CHAS. E. PORTER

Our Ref..................... Your Ref.....................

January 1, 1962

Dear John:

In reply to your enquiry re employment as a junior reporter, I am writing to inform you that I am prepared to offer you the opportunity.

Briefly the position is this: Employment and training as a journalist is subject to three months' satisfactory probation from the time of joining the firm.

The period of probation, which can be ended at any time, by either side, subject to a week's notice, is for your ability to be assessed and for you in turn to satisfy yourself that journalism is suited to your desires and abilities.

If mutual satisfaction results, you will begin work and training under national agreements, including wages and holidays, and every possible encouragement will be given for you to learn the trade in its every department.

As a probationer your starting wage will be £5 10s. gross.

Don't hesitate to give me a ring, or call, if there is anything else you would like to know. Please let me know when you will be able to commence your probation.

Yours truly,
Chas E Porter
Editor

CHAPTER 4

Silly headlines and a lady's bike

It was the late Sixties before I returned to Corporation Street. I had been through a bizarre experience on the Kenilworth Comic, as editor Charlie liked to call it. He had started working life as a Linotype operator (type setting) on the *Telegraph*. He gravitated into journalism after National Service in the RAF.

He was eccentric in the extreme. He was happiest clad in his shorts with ordinary black shoes and socks and vest, cycling the lanes of Warwickshire. His style of writing was also eccentric and would have been unacceptable on most newspapers. But it was fine for the bizarre Comic with his punny and rhyming headlines which were funny (well, they amused me).

In fact we had proof that many people bought the Comic because of Charlie's headlines and I heard many readers chuckling on Midland Red buses.

He would never start a story with the definite (the) or the indefinite (a) article or even a proper noun. This resulted in the most contorted intros (first paragraph) which nearly always came out inverted. I remember one in the splash (front page lead): "In a mood critical were Kenilworth Council on Wednesday night."

As if anyone would talk like that. Then we come to his headlines and these spring to mind:

Car in ditch – broken snitch (driver goes off the road into a ditch and breaks his nose).

He keeps furries at the bottom of his garden (feature on a prize-winning rabbit breeder).

Bear Virgins and Lion reach spicey finale (Story about three pubs: the Bear and Ragged Staff, the Virgins and Castle and the White Lion reaching a darts final. Originally, he had put a comma between Bear and Virgins but asked the stone-hand to chip it off when it was set in metal in the page at the *Courier* printing works in Leamington Spa).

Charlie used to write Pitman's shorthand in huge outlines, probably a rebellion against his time in the RAF, where he was taught to write them in the tiny squares of mathematics paper.

Except for the preview of films coming up the following week at the local cinema, the Alex (where the view from many seats was obscured by pillars), all of the stories in the 28-page newspaper were originated by either Charlie or me.

I had to keep a sense of proportion and taught myself to write in Charlie's style for him but retain what it should really sound like for a proper newspaper. I also became "stuffed up with certificates".

Well, I eventually passed my prized National Council for the Training of Journalists Proficiency Certificate. I could add this to music and swimming qualifications, obviously indispensable to a journalist.

I came to realise later that the best asset a reporter could have, next to being able to report and write, was a language or two. If you were fluent in French or Spanish, you would be at the front of the queue when a big story broke abroad. Without a language, you would have to hire an English-speaking taxi driver.

I had gained my NCTJ Proficiency Certificate after attending day release classes on Fridays at a college in Birmingham. *Courier Press* made me work on Saturday mornings to make up for the time for being away on the Friday, unlike my fellow course members who worked for the *Telegraph*.

I also had to pay for my own Pitman's shorthand lessons (again, unlike the *Telegraph* trainees) and gained a certificate that said I could write it at 100 wpm.

My routine, almost daily, had been to walk to Charlie's home to compare notes on my copy sitting at the dining table in his back room. I had to quickly get used to the free-flying budgerigar that Charlie and his wife always had.

The green-feathered bird would perch on his shoulder as he typed, crapping down his back. It would then fancy a bit of exercise and fly over to sit on my head, still pooping freely. Over the years he had several of these feathered friends, all called Tom. When one fell off its perch it was quickly replaced.

All of Charlie's jackets had traces of Tom's calling card on their shoulders, which didn't seem to bother him. Sartorial elegance was the least of his worries, evidenced by the fact that he rarely took off his bike clips.

Even his evening suit had Tom's calling card and he once arrived on his bike for a very posh Hunt Ball at Thickthorn Manor in Kenilworth and kept his bike clips on throughout the meal and speeches.

Charlie was such a devoted cyclist that he preferred pedal power to using his car, or the wagon, as he would call it. He would pedal for miles giving him craggy, weather-beaten features beneath greying hair which seemed to have the consistency of a Brillo pad.

And I had felt a little disappointed when he told me he had acquired office transport for me. He provided me with a cycle, of course, which would have been fine other than for the fact that it had a lady's frame. I rarely used the bike for fear of being seen by new-found friends in Kenilworth.

Once I had gained invaluable experience and "qualified" as a journalist, I had to think of the future. I was happy at the Comic as I had acquired a number of lady friends. There was Jennifer, a receptionist at the Abbey Hotel opposite the office, and Carol a hairdresser, to name but two.

Anyway, it was time to say goodbye to Charlie, who was a hard but fair taskmaster and I had learned a great deal from him.

I was quite nervous when I plucked up courage to tell him I had been offered a new job at Massey-Ferguson, the tractor company who had a huge production plant in Banner Lane, Coventry, now a housing estate.

And stuck in my mind was a kind note accompanied by 10 shillings – enough to buy about eight pints at the time – placed in a brown envelope from Charlie one Christmas. The note read:

"Dear John. Best wishes for Christmas.

Thanks for your willing help during the year. With your beauty and my bullying, we shall get somewhere - probably the Employment Exchange.
-

CEP"

However, I did quit and was engaged at Massey-Ferguson to produce the company's house magazine, the *Triple Triangle*, but they decided to close it before I arrived. But they honoured the job offer and I ended up doing general PR work and producing *Modern Farmer*, a magazine for customers.

The fact that I was a city boy and knew nothing about farming didn't seem to matter and I joined a product familiarisation course for apprentices at Massey-Ferguson's magnificent school near the Royal Show ground in Stoneleigh, Warwickshire.

I spent three hugely enjoyable weeks tearing around the estate on tractors and combine harvesters and graduated fully briefed about the MF product range.

The move from Hicksville to mixing with senior management at one of the world's biggest businesses was an enormous change. John Keyser (pronounced like the thing you open doors with not as in Kaiser, the German Emperor) was the director of public relations.

John was the most immaculate and polite person I had ever met and I should have known what was coming after I attended my first 8am Monday morning briefing (my clapped out Triumph Courier, bought by my dad, only just managed to get me there on time).

I had turned up in my Kenilworth Comic attire of corduroy jacket and slacks. Don't laugh, corduroy jackets were very *de rigueur* at the time. But my downfall was the flapping Phillips stick-on rubber sole that my dad had attached to my right shoe. John spotted it and had a word in the ear of my immediate boss, John Clews.

He took me to one side and gave me a dressing down before I explained that the transition from weekly pay in cash to monthly by bank transfer had left me a little boracic in the first few weeks of my new employment.

When I told my dad, he marched me into the city and bought me a completely new outfit and wouldn't take the money for it when I got paid at the end of the month.

It was during this time that I met Ann, a PA to the purchasing director at MF, and we were to be married in 1969.

Anyway, things were very short-lived at Banner Lane. After about a year of very enjoyable and leisurely work compared with life on the Kenilworth Comic, I had to move on. A new boss, Peter King, a whiz-kid from London, had succeeded John Keyser and it was curtains for me.

It was a Friday and I was summoned to a meeting at the top of a 14-floor tower block with Peter and Chopper Harris, the legendary hatchet man from human resources. I was being made redundant, given a month's notice and would be paid a month's salary from whenever I managed to get a new job.

I returned to my ground floor office and announced to my colleague Paul Flint what had happened (he was next) and told John Clews I was popping into town to see if I could get a new job.

I arrived at the *Telegraph* office in Corporation Street and asked for Harold Chard, who had been promoted to chief-sub after Harry Reader's departure through retirement or death, I'm not quite sure which.

Harold was very generous, said there was a vacancy on the news subs desk and offered me a job after I assured him that I was fully trained in sub-editing. Not quite true.

He took me to the editor's office and introduced me to John Leese, who confirmed the appointment after in answer to his question I told him my favourite newspaper was the *Daily Mail*.

Probably a good move because John subsequently joined the *Daily Mail* and our paths would cross again when he was charged with closing the *London Evening News*.

I drove back to Banner Lane, told them I had a new job and was starting on Monday. I ripped a half-written story from my portable typewriter, bid them goodbye and headed for the Triumph Courier. It was quite poignant because that typewriter had been bought for my 21st by my mum and dad.

So my second stint at the *Telegraph's* Corporation Street offices was about to start.

Front-page sensation

The front page of the Kenilworth Weekly News from the edition that Lamb edited allowing boss Charlie to go on holiday for the first time in 15 years. The story at top right was a late-breaking drama that was shoe-horned into the front page on the day of publication. Sensational stuff for the Kenilworth Comic. A bomb was never found but this is proof that you should never let the facts spoil a good story.

LOCKE & ENGLAND
Chartered & Estate Auctioneers Agents
Kenilworth
Leamington Spa & Stratford-upon-Avon

The Kenilworth Weekly News

J. & B. TAYLOR
FUNERAL SERVICE
LIMITED
PRIVATE CHAPEL
Tel. Dial 54261 or 26052
PERSONAL ATTENTION
184, WARWICK ROAD

Vol. 18 No. 22 | FRIDAY, AUGUST 21, 1964 | THREEPENCE

Apart Is Way They Want To Stay

ANTI - TOWN ATTITUDE IS KEEN AT BURTON GREEN

UNINVITING to the bulk of Burton Green residents is the prospect of their becoming residents of Kenilworth. Suggestions made by Kenilworth Council in relation to forthcoming boundary reviews, is that those parts of Burton Green at present administered by either Warwick RDC or Meriden RDC, should be transferred to Kenilworth.

But if an opinion poll were taken, it is unlikely that many Burton Green ...

... panded it should put its own clock forward by doing something constructive in its town centre.

"We do not want more Kenilworth, we want less," remarked a resident of long standing. "Remember that car storage and transport nuisance Kenilworth foisted on Burton Green," he said, recalling a long campaign to get rid of an "industry" Kenilworth Council permitted to be established in woodland near the school.

In the main, Burton Green desires to remain rural, become a parish (it has no form of ...

RATE CUTS FOR A FEW

Local people who fall into a certain category will be able to apply to Kenilworth Council for a reduction in their rates.

They must show that their rates have increased by 25 per cent or £5 from March 1963 to March next year, and they are required to produce evidence that they are suffering hardship because of the increase.

Their cases will be looked into by the Council, who will decide whether or not there should be a rate decrease. The survey is being carried out by councils all over the country.

Mr. H. Newell, Kenilworth Council's treasurer, told the KWN that he thought very few people in Kenilworth would fall into the required category because the value of their houses would not have increased sufficiently.

One hundred years of married life. On the left are Mr. and Mrs. Bannard and on the right are Mr. and Mrs. Mason. Both couples this week celebrated their golden wedding anniversary. Story page 4.

BOMB ON GOLF COURSE?

Bomb disposal experts were this week called to Kenilworth Golf Club after reports that there was an unexploded bomb in a stagnant pond near the first tee.

It is known that during the last war a stick of bombs was dropped across the course.

Fresh stories about the existence of a bomb were started after the golf club had drained the pond. They were pumping the water from it to spray the greens.

When the pond was dry they decided to clear the mud out of the bottom of it, and it was then that a nearby resident told the club there was an unexploded bomb in it.

Not wishing to take any risks, the club called in a bomb disposal squad. They have been boring a tube about 15ft. into the earth below the pond and then lowering a detector down it.

So far they have found nothing, but they will continue to bore until they find the bomb or prove conclusively that there is not one in the pond.

There are conflicting stories about the bombs that dropped on the golf course. Some say ...

Photographer's model

Lamb was often called on by a photographer to illustrate a story in the Kenilworth Weekly News. Here he is demonstrating a dangerously overhanging tree in a pathway between Priory Road and Southbank Road in Kenilworth. Such was the trivia that was reported in the news-starved Kenilworth.

Kenilworth Weekly News

Christmas greetings...

...from the boss. A note to Lamb from editor Charlie which was accompanied by a 10s note as a Christmas present.

Dear John,

Best wishes for Christmas.

Thanks for your willing help during the year. With your beauty and my bullying, we shall get somewhere or probably the Employment Exchange.

CEC

Proof positive

A proper qualification at last...Lamb's much-prized proficiency certificate from the National Council for the Training of Journalists awarded in October 1966. It also offered confirmation that he was an exponent of Pitman's shorthand at 100 words a minute.

This

Certificate

in

Practical Journalism

is awarded to

David John Lamb

who has completed the required period of basic training on the staff of the

Kenilworth Weekly News

and has passed the Proficiency Test, reaching the necessary standard in interviewing and reporting, re-writing, current affairs, newspaper practice, newspaper law and shorthand (100 w p m).
The educational requirements of the National Council have also been met.

CHAIRMAN OF THE COUNCIL

DIRECTOR OF THE COUNCIL

EDITOR

October 1966

CHAPTER 5

From news to sport - and the *Pink*

So it was just before Christmas 1967 that I arrived for my first day as a journalist on the *Evening Telegraph* in Corporation Street early on the Monday morning in surroundings that included familiar faces and new ones.

The *Telegraph* was selling 125,000 copies a day – astronomic by today's standards – and it was the City Final edition that was pushed through the letterboxes of many homes in the city.

I took my place at the news subs' table, still T-shaped from my copy boy days, and started work. Across from me was Reg Best.

Now every newspaper subs' table seemed to have a Reg Best. He was not in the full bloom of youth and was, frankly, a cantankerous old bully. If he spotted an indiscretion in a reporter's copy – like the heinous crime of splitting an infinitive – he would loudly announce the crime so that everyone in the office could hear. He would then end his recriminations with "...UP WITH WHICH WE WILL NOT PUT!"

Most of his colleagues ignored him but he seemed to be at his happiest when he was ranting and raving.

We all had to pick stories stacked in a wire tray and usually placed in order of urgency. The page planner would write typographic instructions on the top of the first page – including the size of the headline and the length the story should make when set in type. It would also have the page it was intended for written on the top.

Most of us wanted to come up with a headline that would please chief sub Harold. I remember editing a piece about a letter being delivered in extremely quick time, so I wrote the headline: "***Lick this for post haste!***". It earned a cheer from H.

When our fashion editor (yes, we had such a person!) filed from Paris (yes, we even sent staff abroad!) she was going on about a skirt that was somewhere between a mini and a maxi. So I used the word ***midi*** in the headline and quietly claimed to myself that I invented it (more chief sub cheers).

At lunchtime (half-an-hour) we used to go for a swift pint in the Town Wall Tavern, just across the road from the office, and one of the sports guys told me someone was leaving and that I should apply for the job if I fancied it. He knew that a few years earlier I had worked in the sports room.

I had a word with the Sports Editor Merv "The Swerve" Robilliard, who originated from Jersey. The affable Merv, who had succeeded the unsmiling Jack Canty, offered me the job without hesitation and I duly joined the Sports Desk, which had a totally different working (and drinking) ethic to the news boys.

On the Sport Desk I would be able to expand my experience into page layout, something I was keen to learn, as well as doing some writing. In addition to working on the edition every day, we had to produce the weekly *PINK* edition which went out on Saturday night. Most of the *PINK* pages would be written and prepared for print during the week with five "live" pages kept open for Saturday's action.

I had played rugby at a very junior level for the Keresley Club, which my cousins John and Brian Goss had helped found in 1953 when I was free from work on Saturdays. Despite this, the Telegraph asked me to look after the junior soccer pages in the *PINK*. I was also appointed tennis correspondent, about which I knew less than I did soccer.

Talking of cousin John Goss. He was a talented artist and went on to become a professional photographer in the advertising world. One of his earliest jobs was working on an account for a car that's engine was going to be installed sideways.

Brother Colin and I listened in disbelief. But this was before the Austin Mini was launched and John told us that for the Austin Seven branding he had come up with the idea of turning the V on its side to form a 7. I believe that became the brand for some years.

I was quick to build a good set of contacts in both sports and enjoyed covering them, even resulting in my being sent to cover a day at Wimbledon, which I grew to detest because of its elitism. What other sporting event deliberately makes fans queue through the night in the hope of getting a seat? It never ceases to amaze me that tennis fans are prepared to do this. And another dislike is the way the All England Club pompously calls it "People's Sunday" when they have to arrange play on the middle Sunday.

As a lowly provincial newspaper, we were only allowed a very limited pass and the nearest I could get to the action was standing in the photographers' messenger box on No 1 court.

I wandered into the press area on the Centre Court for a pint and a bite (no way the paper would pay Wimbledon prices for a proper lunch with strawberries and cream) and found most of the tennis hacks watching the action on TV despite the fact that it was taking place in the flesh a few feet away.

I got chatting to the guy from the *Daily Mirror* and he offered his pass so that I could watch a bit of the action from the press box. I climbed the few steps out of the bar and was confronted by an officious-looking gentleman who turned out to be the tennis correspondent of the *London Evening News*.

John Oakley knew I wasn't who I claimed to be and refused me entry. It did, however, cause a laugh when reminded of this when I became his immediate boss on the *Evening News* years later.

My only other taste of big-time tennis was when I covered a Davis Cup match between Great Britain and West Germany at the Edgbaston Priory Club, Birmingham, in 1969.

Again, the *Coventry Evening Telegraph* was a poor cousin compared to the national and Birmingham press. The phone I was to use was hired from an agency. But I was only allowed to make my calls to copy-takers back in Corporation Street at mid-set in the press tent away from the court which rendered the whole exercise in my filing for the *PINK* that night pretty useless (but it made a good piece for Monday's paper).

One of the matches I reported was between Britain's Mark Cox and Wilheim Bungert . But the match was memorable for me by the arrival of a tennis-writing legend, Laurie Pignon, of the *Daily Sketch*.

This larger-than-life character was moustachioed and had a loud clipped accent in the style of Wodehouse. I was so nervous, I had arrived in the press seat in plenty of time but Laurie bustled in late, and as he prepared to sit he turned to those around him and loudly asked: "Anyone got a pen?"

I also managed to get a major scoop in tennis. Ann Jones, from the Edgbaston Priory Club in Birmingham, had won the Wimbledon title in 1969 and I discovered from one of my contacts that she had decided to give up her professional status in order to return to the amateur ranks and play again for Warwickshire.

This was a major story but we couldn't corroborate it with Ann because she was in Switzerland and the editor would not allow me the expense of calling her.

"If you're sure of the story, we'll publish," said John Leese.

No pressure then. We did publish and it really upset the proper tennis correspondent on the *Birmingham Post*, who had cornered all of the Ann Jones stories. He ran a denial without checking with Ann but a few months later she was playing for Warwickshire again.

They must have thought I knew what I was doing on tennis when I successfully tipped the unfancied American Stan Smith to win Wimbledon in 1972. He beat Rumanian Ilie Nastase in a five-set thriller over nearly three hours that became the first final to be played on a

Sunday, having been postponed from the Saturday due to rain. I seem to remember I had managed to get pre-tournament odds of 20-1 on Smith.

But most of my tennis stories were about the local scene. I once covered a county match, featuring talented local players George Holdsworth and Rod Lovegrove, at what was then the newly-opened Beechwood tennis club in Earlsdon, Coventry.

Derek Henderson, our Coventry City FC reporter, was a member and his playing partner was often Joe Elliott, the former chairman of the Sky Blues who was appointed Life-President.

The real excitement was back at the office on Saturday afternoons, especially in the winter and, of course, Coventry City (the Sky Blues) were playing in the top tier, then called Division One.

Saturday was always a hugely busy day but would not prevent us from having a few snifters in the Town Wall Tavern. In fact the editor of the *PINK*, Greg Oliver, was probably the most prolific boozer on the sports desk, who would all have been in the First Division if there were a league for drinking.

He was legendary for every morning at about 9.15 marching off to the gents whistling at the same time with one of the morning papers tucked under his arm. Very regular, was Greg.

After closing time at 2.30, we would return to the office for the kick-offs, which were mostly 3pm. Except Coventry City that is. They had started their home matches at Highfield Road for many years at 3.15.

We decided to ask why because this caused us all sorts of problems trying to get the *PINK* off the stone at 5pm when the City didn't finish until 4.55 at the earliest.

We decided to investigate and it turned out that the City years before had agreed to delay the kick-off because a bus crew shift finished at 3pm at the nearby Harnall Lane bus depot. That gave the crews and the passengers they were carrying time to get to the ground. The bus authority agreed to change and City reverted to 3pm kick-offs, making life a little easier.

My other colleagues on the sports desk were an eclectic bunch. Horse racing editor Reg Mackinnon suffered a catastrophic stroke at his desk but survived for many years, wheelchair-bound.

He was succeeded by Jim Marshall, the desk's statutory Scotsman (there was at least one on every newspaper). He was hugely successful as a tipster despite rarely having been on a racecourse and won the *Sporting Life* tipster of the year competition.

Jim had arrived from Glasgow and was always short of money, frequently asking if you could spare him "a pound or two".

Early on I had lent him half-a-crown. The investment held me in good stead because I refused to give him any more until that was repaid. But Jim reformed and went on to have a long career on the *Telegraph*.

He had a stutter, particularly in drink. It became a problem for him when he was invited to join his sports desk colleagues for a drinking session in Whittleford, near Nuneaton.

When the conductor came for the fare, Jim said he wanted to get off at "W-w---w---w---w--- oh, fuck it, Nuneaton!".

An early acquaintance on the Sport Desk was Charlie Tibballs, a journeyman journalist who used to look after the race and dog cards and rarely got involved in anything remotely creative.

On my first day on the sports desk, he accompanied me to the canteen for lunch, where I experienced something that has never left my mind since. He had retrieved his false teeth from his desk drawer in order to eat and after the meal he proceeded to lick them clean at the table.

But I grew to love working on the *Telegraph* and particularly the *PINK*, mainly because I was often charged with writing the front page "splash" headline. I became particularly adept at composing punny headlines (probably a result of my formative years with Charlie Porter). The editor had banned corny headlines expect for the front of the *PINK*. He gave **WIN AND TONIC** as an acceptable example.

I made many friends, a lot of them printers, having taken Charlie Porter's advice that they could be your best friend or worst enemy. They certainly wielded all the power then.

Chewing the fat over lunch...

The Telegraph canteen in all its glory with the ladies preparing lunch. It was at one of those tables that was the scene of Lamb's lunch with sports desk colleague, Charlie Tibballs. After devouring his fish and chips, he took out his false teeth and licked them clean. An experience never to be forgotten.

Mirrorpix

Foul!

John Lamb takes out the opposition goalkeeper, as instructed, in a match between the Telegraph's editorial and advertising departments. The game took place at the newspaper's magnificent sports ground off Lythalls Lane in Coventry and was one of the many leading Coventry companies that had superb sports facilities.

CHAPTER 6

Sport and strife

Coventry was thriving in the early part of the Seventies as a major contributor to the UK being the second biggest car manufacturer in the world. The huge car plants of Jaguar, British Leyland (which included the Triumph, Rover and Jaguar marques) and Rootes Group (later Chrysler and the Peugeot) were churning out thousands of models every day.

There were also Massey-Ferguson, Dunlop, Alvis and Courtaulds (which had a county-standard cricket pitch at their sports ground in Lockhurst Lane) plus huge employers like Coventry Gauge and Tool, Alfred Herbert and Renold Chain.

The average wage in Coventry at that time was about 25 per cent higher than the rest of the UK but that sadly plummeted with the decline of the car industry in the late Seventies and early Eighties.

Most of these companies had magnificent sports grounds and the Telegraph was among them. They had an oasis in the urban area of the Foleshill district in the city. It had a clubhouse and was surrounded by poplar trees.

In the middle was a cricket square and a soccer pitch and the ground was run by a combination of management and staff. Some of the takings from the bar back in Corporation Street were used to help finance it, I believe.

At the *Telegraph* building in Corporation Street there was also a club. In the early days it was on the floor above the editorial subs' room, also overlooking Belgrade Square.

The bar adjoined the canteen and was open at lunchtimes and in the evening. Table tennis was also available and what became a very competitive tournament was introduced.

During my first stint as a copy boy at the *Telegraph* I spent much of my time in the bar with my pal Ralph Dolby and we got to know most of the regulars there. They included non-*Telegraph* people who were allowed to join as associate members.

Many a riotous night took place there where the world was put to rights with me and Ralph always arguing the toss. Anyway, making friends with the hacks who drank there did me no harm when I was seeking work later.

Drinking was a big part of the culture at all newspapers and it was rare to find a teetotaller among your colleagues.

Unlike most newspapers today, the *Telegraph* was part of the fabric of the city. The *Coventry Evening Telegraph* Cup was much sought-after by leading soccer teams in the area. There were junior and minor cups and the *Telegraph* supported all manner of sports, including professional golf tournaments like the Warwickshire Open.

We also had a golf team for an annual match against the *Birmingham Post and Mail*. My debut was in a match played at the Forest of Arden, then a new course, between the Coventry and Birmingham elements of the Iliffe empire – so a convenient venue for everyone.

We lined up on the first tee in pairs and the opposition included Tim Morris, a very senior manager who became managing director of the *Coventry Evening Telegraph* and later moved to Birmingham in a similar role.

He, of course, drove first. He sliced his shot badly and it was heading for a pond on the right when his ball hit a thin marker post and bounced back into the middle of the fairway.

Tim turned to us and said in his very public school accent: "You know, you don't reach the upper echelon of management without a little bit of luck." We marched off down the fairway cursing and muttering something about silver spoons.

The relationship between management and staff was generally brilliant but fraught at times. Infrequent strikes did happen but not as regular as those in the car factories. Industrial strife was rarely off the front page of the Telegraph in the belief that workers wanted to bury their heads in the stories when they had been working among it all day.

In my experience, they turned away from this continual stream of strife and immediately went to the back of the paper for the soccer and the horse racing.

When I joined the *Telegraph* at Quinton Road, the printers had just settled strike action. A much-reduced newspaper was produced by the non-striking journalists, causing bitterness among the inkies that was never far from the surface afterwards.

So a few years later when we had moved into Corporation Street and we National Union of Journalists members went on strike for more pay, the printers carried on working. The editor and some of his senior colleagues managed to produce a much-reduced newspaper.

We didn't actually call it a strike. We arranged a series of "mandatory meetings" at the headquarters of the Amalgamated Engineering Union just down the road from the Telegraph in Corporation Street.

Sadly, this also caused strife among colleagues. After spending a couple of days in a smoke-filled room with my colleagues, I developed a horrible cold so didn't go to the "mandatory" session. Apart from the fact that I was bored to tears, I did not want to spread germs among my revolutionary brothers.

But my wife, Ann, who was at work, needed money for food so I wrapped up and drove to the bank in Corporation Street – next to the AEU office. News editor Les Chamberlain spotted me and he brought my actions to the notice of the meeting.

I was hauled up before the committee to explain why I had become a blackleg. It was a joke, of course. Rather like the way the management treated a remark by my sports desk colleague, rugby reporter Bob Phillips, when we invited management to a meeting of the Chapel, as NUJ branches were and still are called.

The top man was the Father of the Chapel and he called on Bob, who by then had been elevated to a senior union position, to speak. He caused uproar when he suggested that worker representation on the company board was "a couple of years away".

Management couldn't stop laughing but I imagine their attitudes would be very different in today's world of working relationships.

We were also required to picket the office to try to influence the inkies and working journalists to join us. I seem to remember the picket turned into an urban streets cricket match. Like most NUJ-inspired strikes it all came to nothing and we returned to work no better off than when we had started.

There were also problems of a different kind for me. My phone rang on the sports desk and when I answered a female voice said: "Did you get him?"

"What are you talking about?" I asked.

"The guy who you asked me to keep talking while he spoke in obscene terms so that you could trace the call," she said.

I genuinely did not have a clue what she was talking about. But on further questioning she said she had received a call from someone purporting to be me (I guess my name was fairly well known in the area at the time).

He told the lady that we had received a tip from the police following her advertisement for a flat-mate saying we understood she was going to receive an obscene call. He asked her not to hang up because the police wanted to trace the call.

Obviously, the same guy called back and got whatever satisfaction perverts like that derive from making obscene calls. We concluded that he trawled the ads in the *Telegraph* looking for advertisements which were obviously placed by a female and would call in my name.

We ran a warning in the paper and then one day I had a call from the front office saying that two police officers wanted to see me. When I joined them in the meeting room off reception, I walked in and foolishly said: "I know what you've come about."

They looked at each other and I'm sure they thought I was bang to rights. Anyway, I convinced them I was innocent. The calls continued until an acquaintance, who I suspected, was killed in a car crash. The calls stopped.

I also learned a valuable lesson. A friend of mine called to say his mother had been caught shoplifting and could I keep it out of the paper? I asked him to tell me nothing about the case because the chances were that nothing would go in the paper for such a minor offence.

It didn't but I hoped he didn't think I had anything to do with it not appearing.

One of the Telegraph's great characters - photographer Bob Cole. Bob and Lamb regularly worked together covering Coventry rugby matches at Coundon Road. Bob played rugby and cricket himself and was a talented batsman. He is pictured celebrating another victory in front of the pavilion at the Telegraph's sports ground in Lythalls Lane, Coventry, which closed in 2003.

Bob Cole

Misspent youth...

Being a good snooker player indicates a misspent youth, they say. Certainly true in these cases - Bob (left) and Lamb's sports desk colleague Ken Widdows with friend before getting down to some serious potting.

Bob Cole

Library with a difference...

Library personnel hard at work on the second floor of the Telegraph's Corporation Street headquarters. This was a vital part of the newspaper's operations where cuttings of stories used in all editions and pictures were filed.

If a reporter was writing a story about a person, an incident, a death, an accident, indeed anything that might have a history of stories, he or she would call the library and ask for the "cuts" and pictures. Lamb would then be dispatched to fetch the material and deliver to the reporter's desk.

Mirrorpix

CHAPTER 7

Using the technology of Dickens

In today's digital world, it's probably apposite to explain how newspapers were produced during most of my time in the *Telegraph's* Corporation Street offices. The technology used at this time was not enormously different to that employed to produce *Household Words*, an English weekly magazine edited by Charles Dickens in the 1850s. It took its name from the line in Shakespeare's Henry V: "Familiar in his mouth as household words."

These were really the first "soaps" with Dickens telling a story in episodes that had such a heady climax you could not resist buying next week's edition.

The *Telegraph* production process, like most major evening newspapers at the time, started with the words and pictures pouring into the office from reporters, agencies like the Press Association, and freelance journalists.

We often used to have parties from schools visiting the office and on one occasion a pupil asked one of the best questions I have heard about newspapers. She wanted to know how it was that there was just enough news to fill the newspaper every day.

I explained to her that only about 15 per cent of the information that came into the office every day actually made it into the newspaper and added that it was down to the skills of journalists to ensure that everything readers should know was included.

All of the words and the pictures would be dealt with by page planners and sub-editors, deciding which were the best stories and photographs (called "tasting") and giving them appropriate prominence on the page plan, which would be drawn on sheets of paper with just the columns marked on them. You would be told if the pages had advertisements.

Much the same process prevails today, except the words and pictures arrive digitally on screens rather than on paper and in hard pictures.

The stories would be sent to the printers to be set into type. There would never be more than two paragraphs on a sheet of copy-paper so that the stories could be spread around several composing machines. Even the longest stories would be set in type in minutes.

The edited copy would also have setting instructions on each page. The intro might be 12-point Century bold across two columns; the second paragraph 10pt Century light, also across two columns; and the rest of the copy 7pt across one column.

The skill of the sub-editor involved assessing how much the story would make when set in type. He would be told by the page-planner that three inches across two columns and eight inches across one column were required. You would insert the occasional crosshead (a small headline) to break up a long run of type.

The headline instructions would be something like two lines of 42pt Century bold caps across four columns. The sub would know how many letters could be used because, unlike today's digital systems, you could not stretch metal type.

The sub would be practised in counting an "l" as a half letter along with all the other narrow letters in lowercase. Ms and Ws would count as one-and-a-half.

There was a little leeway by reducing the spacing between the letters but generally you were stuck with the "count", as it was called. Sometimes you would get the headline back from the printers with "BUST" written across it, which meant that it did not fit.

This was frowned upon, because problems like this would only delay the process. Every page had a time for when it must be finished. Features pages would be completed overnight and then each later news and sports page would have a time by which it should be completed.

Today, newspapers restrict the amount of squeezing and stretching now possible with digital technology in order not to change the character of the end product.

The first pages were assembled in metal frames called "chases", as they were called, with adjustable edges. Once all the type was in and everything fitted, bolts fitted into the edges of the chase would be tightened.

Occasionally, if the page had not been made up square, it would "burst" with type flying all over the place. I only saw that happen twice, and on one occasion it happened because the stonehand (not at the *Telegraph*) was drunk and had not made up the page properly.

The metal bench on which the page was made up was called the stone and every page had an "off the stone" time. The front and back would be the last to go, with other pages being sent to the presses earlier in ten-minutes intervals.

Between being set in type and the stone, the type would be assembled on long thin trays know as galleys. Ink would then be applied to the type and a proof on long strips of plain newsprint taken. It would then be rolled up in the copy and sent to the readers' boxes.

These were a row of small cubicles populated by a copyreader and a copyholder. One would read the words written by the reporter and edited by the sub and the words would be checked against the printer's proof.

The copyreader would use a set of hieroglyphics to correct the copy and then that was sent back to the printers for only the lines with errors to be put right.

The bundle of correction lines, along with the copy, would then be sent to the stone along with the copy for the new lines to be dropped into the page and those with the errors discarded.

If time was pressing, the stone-hand, or more likely his boss, would try to press the "stone sub" (the journalist nominated to be on the stone that day) that the page had been corrected and was ready to go.

But you could always tell if a story had been corrected because the lines, which had replaced the original type, would not have ink on them. It was rare for a story not to contain some corrections.

The demarcation rules were very strong in the composing room with no non-print union personnel allowed to touch the type. There was some commonsense behind this rule because if everyone was allowed to wander around picking up type, chaos would have resulted.

I only ever witnessed one "printers pie" – the name for the result of a printer dropping a galley of type and, incidentally, the name of a famous pub in Fleet Street. This involved the football pools guide for the *PINK* edition of the *Telegraph*. It was a delicate construction of single pieces of type giving the noughts and crosses for the football pools based on the results that day. It was about 12 inches deep and a column wide, wrapped in a piece of string.

It was always the last item to be added to the back page of the *PINK* and on this night it ended up on the floor in a horrible mess. However, there was always a lovely sense of the theatre in newspapers and the problem was quickly put right and we printed only a few minutes late.

To mitigate against such an accident we would have prepared a "house" advertisement to take the place of the demolished pools guide.

This all seems terribly archaic compared with today's printing methods where pages are made up and completed on computer screens.

The end product looks much cleaner but I still hanker for the dramatic days of hot metal with the familiar smells and noises of the composing room. There were days when some of the smells were rather unwelcome after the printers had been on a Black Country night out which included gallons of the wonderful Batham's bitter and faggots and peas.

Ready for 'the off...'

Drivers of the Telegraph's fleet of vans poised to rush the next edition to readers in Coventry and beyond. There were seven editions and day so is was important they made their journeys as quickly as possible. In bad weather, the whole operation would switch to "snow times" with just one edition covering all areas. The bundles of papers used to arrive from the press room on a conveyor belt through the doors on the left.

Mirrorpix

Front of house...

Two of the Telegraph advertising personnel when the front office was busy with callers trying to sell cars and houses and much more. Many readers would also announce family milestones with births, marriages and deaths (known as BMDs or hatched, matched and dispatched).

CHAPTER 8

The Pink - 1

In the late Sixties and Seventies the *PINK* Saturday night sports edition sold a fluctuating number of copies. I don't recall the exact figures but it was about 15,000 if the Sky Blues lost at home rising to about 30,000 if they won away. In later years, with Coventry City playing on a variety of days, the *PINK* was closed. It was just not economically viable if the Sky Blues did not have a match.

But the *PINK* is still talked of in revered terms. Everyone seems to remember waiting at their paper shop for the *PINK* to be thrown on to the pavement outside and then bundled on to the counter for sale. It also sold well in the pubs and clubs.

I recently found an old edition, saved by my father, in which I had written the front page headline on Coventry City's away match with Newcastle United on Saturday, March 29, 1969.

Soccer reporter Derek Henderson wrote that City had been beaten by two goals scored from corners, so my headline was:

CITY CORNERED BY MAGPIES

This was when Saturday night sports editions were a cracking read, printed within half-an-hour of matches ending. As well as the Sky Blues' report, the front page on this night included a short story and the 1,2,3,4 of the Grand National, an FA Cup semi-final report, full classified Football League results and up-to-date league tables. A great achievement produced within minutes of the final whistles.

The *PINK* in its earlier days was famous for the pseudonyms it gave its writers, rather than using their proper names for by-lines.

I guess the logic was that it gave the reports anonymity and any views expressed to be taken as those of the publication and not an individual. NEMO ("The Man") was Derek Henderson; NIMROD ("Skilful Hunter") the rugby correspondent David Irvine; FLEETFOOT did athletics; LEFT GUARD boxing; JACK O'GREEN crown green bowls; and DOUBLE TOP darts. One of the earlier NIMRODs had been the grumpy news sub-editor Reg Best.

I'm not sure that they extended any further than that. But speedway was a big sport and the reporter could, I suppose, have been LEG TRAILER.

I don't think there was a pseudonym for the swimming guy either. BREAST STROKE? I always thought it odd that Bob Phillips, the rugby reporter who doubled at swimming, could not swim.

But I'm pretty sure that was and is the case for many sports reporters and I'm certain LEFT GUARD had never pulled on boxing gloves in anger.

Derek Henderson doubled as FLEETFOOT, which always attracted derision from the players when he boarded the Sky Blues' team bus for an away match This courtesy of travelling with the players was introduced by publicity-savvy Jimmy Hill, the innovative manager of the Sky Blues who took them from obscurity to the First Division.

The Saturday routine was that the *PINK* had to be off the stone by 4.55pm so that the inkies could finish their shift at 5pm, depriving them of overtime. The journalists enjoyed no such potential privileges.

So out in the subs' room we would edit the copy as it was filed from the big games – Coventry City, Coventry Rugby, and the top Midlands matches. Coventry Rugby, or Cov, was the premier team in England, arguably in Wales too.

But that was in pre-league days when Cov had one of the strongest club fixture lists in the country. At one time they boasted 11 internationals on their books.

For most weeks, the Sky Blues were the main story. Derek Henderson coined the Sky Blues nickname when they were promoted to the First Division. They first wore their new colours in a pre-season friendly against Birmingham City.

Derek had joined the *Telegraph* in 1958 and he was NEMO until 1964, when Coventry City were promoted to the First Division for the first time in their history. He was the last NEMO and no trace of the identity of his predecessors can be found. The strange *Telegraph* tradition of hiding their sports columnists gradually ended over the next few years.

Derek would dictate his story from the press box to a copytaker. His words would then be rushed to me (or whoever was editing the lead on that day). A maximum of two paragraphs were allowed for each page and as the game progressed the copy was rapidly set into type in the composing room, sped there in the same tubes I had used as a copy boy.

So by the time the final whistle went, all Derek had to do was write an intro on the result and I had to write the headline. I would be given a "count" by *PINK* editor Greg – that was the number of letters in caps at about 170 point that he had left in his page design, which was often done at the last minute to allow a good headline to be accommodated.

The front page was busy with the start of the City match report (it would turn to an inside page), the classified results and league tables. The pace was pretty frenetic and everyone was busy, with more than one story to look after. There were occasions when I subbed the rugby as well as the City match.

But most of my colleagues and I loved it. I was tense when I was first given the job of sub-editing the lead. It was a demanding time and you strove to come up with the most eye-catching headline while dealing with the story and other items.

One of the first times I was given the Sky Blues game to handle for the PINK was on Saturday, December 7, 1968, when they played Queens Park Rangers at Loftus Road.

Greg had given me a count of about 10 capital letters for the two-deck headline.

Coventry took the lead through a Willie Carr volley in the third minute so they had a long time to hang on and I had to wait to write the headline. As the game progressed and City stayed in the lead, I sent the headline to the printers. I wrote **CARR DRIVES CITY AHEAD** in two lines. I thought I would have to re-write the headline when QPR were awarded a penalty.

Derek Henderson wrote: "Nine minutes from the end, Marsh (Rodney) was awarded a penalty when he was tackled by Martin. It looked like a blatant 'dive' by the Rangers' man but the referee pointed to the spot and though the kick was not taken for several moments Marsh finally took it. He took a strange looking diagonal run at the ball and hit it outside the right-hand upright to the groans of the Rangers' fans."

In his comment on the front page, Derek described Marsh's actions as "one of the most theatrical pieces of diving I have seen on a football field in years, with Marsh doing a dying swan act as he was challenged by Martin".

So I was sweating on my headline until the very last minute but when the final whistle went and we had won, I changed **AHEAD** to **HOME** and that got me the job regularly.

One of my other favourite headlines was when Rochdale, Third Division relegation candidates, knocked City out of the FA Cup in a third-round match at their Spotland ground on Monday, January 11, 1971.

"City were behind after 39 minutes to a Cross header," wrote Derek, "but though Hunt equalised six minutes after the break the Sky Blues failed to get a grip and Butler scored the winner 10 minutes from time."

I wrote: **BUTLER SERVES CUP KO**

The game was played on a Monday afternoon because the tie had been postponed through bad weather and Spotland didn't have adequate lights for a night match.

For most seasons, Coventry were involved in a relegation battle and when the crunch game came we would prepare the headline for the front page in advance.

We would have **SAFE!** or **DOWN!** in the largest type you could imagine. But the superstitious printers would not place the headline into the page until the match was over. For many years, it was SAFE! until the Sky Blues were eventually relegated in 2001 after 34 years in the top tier.

Noel Cantwell had been appointed manager of Coventry City in 1967 in succession to the legendary Jimmy Hill, who had taken the club to the First Division for the first time.

One of my most wasted days was spent hiding with a photographer in a car outside Noel's house trying to prove that he was talking to Manchester City's Malcolm Allison about joining him at Highfield Road.

Allison did, indeed, turn up but wouldn't answer my questions when I confronted him and the story remained as it started life – a rumour.

In fact I was the cause of Noel falling out big time with the *Telegraph*. Derek was always writing about the poor gates at Highfield Road and had composed yet another inquest into why fans were not watching in greater numbers.

We always used to tell Derek that the answer to falling gates was stronger hinges. He never appreciated the joke.

I laid out a feature page for Derek's latest inquest into poor gates and wanted a picture of Noel looking miserable. I found one in the *Telegraph* library file with him downcast, hands deep in the pockets of his trench coat, in the changing room in the stand after it had been damaged by fire.

It fitted the story perfectly, and I did a cut-out of Noel, taking out the background of burnt-out timbers and other debris. He was not best pleased and he banned Derek from the team coach in revenge even though our man tried to explain it was not his decision to use that picture.

Friday back pages were normally full of Coventry City team news so that week we, in retaliation, led on something else and used just two paragraphs at the bottom of the page announcing nothing more than the Sky Blues team and that of their opponents.

Derek was soon back in his regular seat on the team bus. We generally had good relationships with the players and I joined a committee which included City players Willie Carr and Ernie Hunt to raise money for a youngster whose junior playing career had been ended by serious injury in a car crash.

The three of us would meet to discuss fund-raising tactics at the Royal Oak pub, in Earlsdon, my local to this day. They would draw up in their E-type Jaguars – me in my now even more ailing Triumph Courier.

The Pink - 1

A selection of front page "splash" headlines written by Lamb for the Saturday sports edition the PINK. These were written under great pressure to meet the print deadline, which was only 10 minutes after the matches had finished.

BUTLER SERVES CUP KO*: This was a PINK football special on Monday, January 11, 1971. City's FA Cup third round match at Rochdale's Spotland ground had been postponed from Saturday through of an unfit pitch and was played in the afternoon because they did not have adequate lights. Lamb had to wait until the 80th minute to write this headline when winger Dennis Butler scored a shock winner for the Third Division relegation candidates to dump their First Division opponents out of the FA Cup.*

CARR DRIVES CITY HOME*: Lamb had to sweat for 87 minutes before he could be certain of this headline on Saturday, December 7, 1968. Willie Carr scored after three minutes against fellow First Division strugglers Queens Park Rangers at Loftus Road. Without knowing the result, Lamb initially wrote: CARR DRIVES CITY AHEAD. But on the final whistle and seconds from deadline he changed AHEAD to HOME.*

OH BOY! IT'S O'ROURKE*: Coventry took a team depleted through injury to White Hart Lane for a league clash with Tottenham. They came from behind to win 2-1 with John O'Rourke scoring the decisive goal in the 81st minute. Martin Peters scored in the 13th minute on his debut for Spurs after his transfer from West Ham. The PINK had started using the cartoon figure called Sky Blue Sam, created by cartoonist Mick, to reflect the mood of the result.*

Coventry Evening Telegraph

FOOTBALL

No 24,725 MONDAY JANUARY 11 1971 6d

George Best . . . suspended by club.

Best misses showdown —banned

MANCHESTER UNITED directors today suspended Irish international George Best for 14 days.

BUTLER SERVES CUP K O

ROCHDALE 2 COVENTRY CITY 1

COVENTRY CITY were today the victims of a sensational third round of the FA Cup when Rochdale—among the relegation candidates in the Third Division—knocked them out in front of a delirious 13,000 crowd at Spotland.

City were behind after 39 minutes to a Cross header but though Hunt equalised six minutes after the break the Sky Blues failed to get a grip and Butler scored the winner 10 minutes from time.

Derek Henderson reports from Spotland

SPORT IN SHORT

Coventry Evening Telegraph

PINK FINAL

No 24,475 SATURDAY MARCH 21 1970 5d

Results, tables

DIVISION I			
Burnley	2	West Brom.	1
Chelsea	2	Man. Utd.	1
Derby	3	Crystal P.	1
Ipswich	2	Sunderland	0
Liverpool	0	Everton	2
Man. City	1	West Ham	5
Newcastle	3	Stoke City	1
Sheff. Wed.	2	Nottm. F.	1
Southampton	0	Arsenal	2
Tottenham	1	Coventry	2
Wolves	1	Leeds Utd.	2

DIVISION II			
Aston Villa	1	Blackburn	1
Bolton W.	1	Charlton	1
Bristol City	3	Swindon	3
Carlisle	1	Blackpool	2
Huddersfield	2	Birmingham	0
Leicester C.	2	Sheff. Utd.	1
Middlesbro'	0	Norwich	0
Millwall	2	Hull	1
Oxford U.	0	Q.P.R.	0
Preston	1	Portsmouth	2
Watford	2	Cardiff	1

OH BOY! IT'S O'ROURKE

TOTTENHAM 1 COVENTRY CITY 2

COVENTRY CITY'S patched up team went to London optimistically today, but surprised even their own supporters by coming from behind against Tottenham to grab two second half goals and chalk up their 8th away victory of the season.

The Sky Blues looked booked for a rough passage when Martin Peters headed an early goal on his debut, but new skipper Neil Martin and John O'Rourke scored the goals that keep their side in the European picture.

One down, then City heroes battle back

Sky Blue Sam says: "What a spur for Europe!"

VERDICT

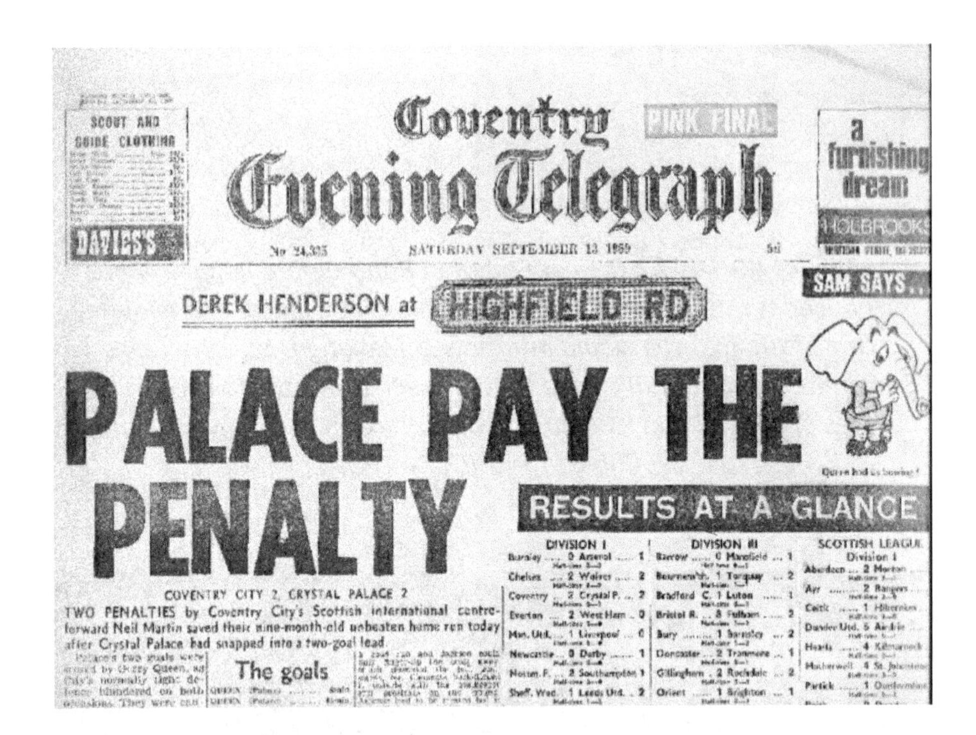

SCOUT AND GUIDE CLOTHING — DAVIES'S

Coventry Evening Telegraph

PINK FINAL

a furnishing dream — HOLBROOKS

No 24,335 SATURDAY SEPTEMBER 13 1969 5d

DEREK HENDERSON at HIGHFIELD RD

SAM SAYS...

Queen had us bowing!

PALACE PAY THE PENALTY

COVENTRY CITY 2, CRYSTAL PALACE 2

TWO PENALTIES by Coventry City's Scottish international centre-forward Neil Martin saved their nine-month-old unbeaten home run today after Crystal Palace had snapped into a two-goal lead.

The goals

RESULTS AT A GLANCE

DIVISION I	DIVISION III	SCOTTISH LEAGUE Division I
Burnley ... 0 Arsenal ... 1	Barrow ... 0 Mansfield ... 1	Aberdeen ... 2 Morton ...
Chelsea ... 2 Wolves ... 2	Bournem'th. 1 Torquay ... 2	Ayr ... 2 Rangers ...
Coventry ... 2 Crystal P. ... 2	Bradford C. 1 Luton ... 1	Celtic ... 1 Hibernian ...
Everton ... 2 West Ham ... 0	Bristol R. ... 3 Fulham ... 2	Dundee Utd. 5 Airdrie ...
Man. Utd. ... 1 Liverpool ... 0	Bury ... 1 Barnsley ... 2	Hearts ... 4 Kilmarnock ...
Newcastle ... 0 Derby ... 1	Doncaster ... 2 Tranmere ... 1	Motherwell 4 St. Johnstone ...
Nottm. F. ... 2 Southampton 1	Gillingham . 2 Rochdale ... 2	Partick ... 1 Dunfermline ...
Sheff. Wed. 1 Leeds Utd. ... 2	Orient ... 1 Brighton ... 1	

CHANEL for CHRISTMAS at WELTONS 13 HIGH STREET

Coventry Evening Telegraph

PINK FINAL

You must see our WONDERFUL SELECTION of CHRISTMAS GIFTS — Holbrooks

No 21,098 SATURDAY DECEMBER 7 1968 5d

CARR DRIVES CITY HOME!

Bill Glazier, City's 'keeper, makes a daring save at the feet of Rodney Marsh, with Dave Clements on hand.

QP RANGERS 0 COVENTRY CITY 1

Derek Henderson at Loftus Road

A THIRD minute goal by young Scot Willie Carr gave Coventry City a much-needed victory in London today over fellow strugglers Queens Park Rangers. Rodney Marsh, Ranger's No 10 missed an 81st minute penalty.

RESULTS AT A GLANCE

DIVISION I	SCOTTISH LEAGUE Division I	DIVISION IV
Arsenal ... 3 Everton ... 1	Aberdeen ... 2 Hibernian ... 5	Bradford C. 1 North'n Co. ... 1
		Grimsby ... 2 Rochdale ... 0

Cov-Moseley do battle...

One of the key fixtures at Coundon Road before leagues were introduced was the biannual match between Coventry and Moseley. One of the fixtures would alternate on Boxing Day. Here Cov's England international centre Peter Preece attempts to escape the clutches of John Finlan. Looking on are Malcolm Swain (Moseley) and Bob Griffiths (Coventry).

Ken Kelly

CHAPTER 9

The Pink - 2

I would often deputise for the rugby reporters, first Bob Phillips and then Michael Austin, when they were elsewhere covering internationals, regional representative matches or on holiday. This mostly involved reporting on matches at the Coventry home ground, Coundon Road.

I was privileged to get to know most of the Cov players personally and they included England internationals David Duckham, Keith Fairbrother, Peter Preece, Geoff Evans, Alan Cowman, Peter Rossborough, John Barton, Fran Cotton, Rodney ("Sam") Webb, Bill Gittings, Barry Ninnes, Barrie Corless, Chris Wardlow and Welsh cap Ron Jones.

Other good friends were John Gray and John Gallagher, both hookers, back row forward Richard Walker, winger Simon Maisey and later scrum-half Steve Thomas. Another huge character was Irish international scrum-half Colin Grimshaw.

There were some memorable away matches, which completely wiped out the weekend. We would return in the small hours if we weren't staying over and Monday's analysis piece had to be written on Sunday.

But post-match was always a party, except for Alan Cowman, who regularly stayed on the coach studying, or at least reading, while we got hammered.

New Brighton, although not in the same league in terms of talent as Cov, was one of the favourite away trips. This was still before leagues were established, which ironically was something the then boss of Cov, Alf Wyman, campaigned for.

When it came, Coventry could not cope with professionalism and have languished in the lower leagues ever since. But that's another story.

New Brighton always put on a party and on one occasion both Coventry teams played in the north-west because Coventry's home ground at Coundon Road was unfit through ice on the pitch.

I covered the first team game live from the press box and paid a youngster £1 to go behind the stand to find out what was going on in the Extras' (second team) match so that I could file that report for the *PINK* too.

After the match, I had a quick shower, went to the coach to write my Monday piece and returned fresh to the clubhouse for a good night out.

When I joined the Cov players, they were playing a disciplinary game which involved drinking with one pre-determined hand and many other daft rules I can't remember. Duckham was in the chair when about five pints of bitter landed on me and the guys next to me.

I took the brunt of a tray thrown for some inexplicable reason by one of the New Brighton players. In fairness he was pretty pissed but it all seemed a terrible waste.

While I was drying every stitch of my clothing, including a very fashionable suede coat, in the hand-dryer in the gents, the Cov players took retribution. They grabbed the culprit, turned him upside down and shook every coin and note out of his pockets, which bought us several rounds during the evening.

During the course of it, there was much activity in the darkened stand as some of players and others got to know the local talent much better.

Dirty games unfit for the parlour were very much a part of the rugby scene then. I will mention just one with a warning that this is really unfit for a publication designed for family reading.

We were at Wasps ground Sudbury in London and it involved nominating a player from each team who would attempt to displace the most beer from a pint pot filled to the brim by lowering their manhood into it.

The loser would be forced to drink both pints. I can't remember Coventry ever losing at this little competition because on their team they had the very well-endowed back row forward.

Talking of Wasps, who now have their home at the Ricoh Arena in Coventry, this visit went down in notoriety in the annals of Coventry Rugby Club.

After the bollock-dunking competition, the Wasps team drifted away and the Cov players started chatting up the very camp barmen. While they were distracted, other Cov players cleaned out the bar of its spirits and other drinks.

The haul, including one of those huge whiskey bottles in which people would save change, was stashed in the ditch at the side of the drive. Driver Tex was instructed to hide them among the kit in the coach boot.

Huge recriminations took place between the clubs but peace broke out eventually. It was decided to consume the booty in a huge piss-up when the clubs next met.

Talking of coach boots, there is another tale from these times which should be recorded. A rugby player from New Zealand had joined Cov and accompanied them on an away match to Wales.

The Cov players convinced him that he needed his passport to get across the Welsh "border". He confessed that he did not have the document so they made him hide in the boot with the kit while they loudly acted out a scene at the fictitious border.

They did the same on the return journey, having sworn the player to say nothing once they were in Wales. We can suppose that there is now a former rugby player wandering around New Zealand in the belief that there is a border control between England and Wales.

I used a sports diary I wrote in the *Telegraph* to defend the questionable alleged antics of one of Coventry's key players, England international prop Keith Fairbrother.

Coventry had drawn 19-19 with Bridgend at Coundon Road and when one of the very merry visiting supporters, Neville Walsh, admonished Keith for not clapping the team off the Coventry prop forward allegedly rounded on him and spat in his eye. Keith always denied the accusation.

But the incident caused uproar in the stand and the victim, a distinguished lawyer and raconteur in Port Talbot, complained to the Rugby Union and demanded an apology.

I wrote a piece in my column, called Sportstalk, not condoning Keith's apparent actions but suggesting spectators should stay clear of players still fired up directly after the match.

My column contributed to Keith and the lawyer kissing and making up and the incident was buried.

Merv the Swerve always had a sharp eye for the opposite sex and a very attractive and mature tea lady did not escape his leer. She would visit the office at least twice a day, dispensing tea from an urn perched on a trolley. You could always hear it coming as her chariot laden with cups rattled into the office.

Purely by happenchance, I'm sure, Merv found himself in the same office lift as the lady and her tea trolley.

They started groping between the side of the lift and the tea trolley and apparently managed a knee-trembler with Merv keeping one finger on the door-close button.

I've no reason to doubt this story because Merv recounted it many times when he had had a drink. But the second bit might be apocryphal.

Legend had it that when they were in the clinches, Merv's finger slipped off the button and the doors opened on the second-floor management suite. The red-faced and dishevelled couple were, allegedly, confronted with senior *Telegraph* figures who had broken for lunch after a long board meeting.

This floor included owner Lord Iliffe's flat complete with butler. Very few personnel ever ventured into this hallowed area except when senior management would be attending a board meeting in the adjoining boardroom.

This whole area was sumptuously decorated in wooden panels (I'm not sure what the wood was but it looked expensive). This décor has survived and I understand will be used as part of the hotel.

One of my duties in my previous life as a copy boy was to take that morning's Times to the flat. I often wondered if the butler ironed it before presenting the paper to his Lordship.

So, after this minor indiscretion Merv, sadly, departed the scene, although I'm not sure that it was entirely down to his tryst with the tea lady. It was the sort of thing you got promoted for in those days but he left to edit the Coventry City FC programme. He then established a news agency in Nuneaton.

Happy Christmas to all our readers

The sports desk, as seen by cartoonist Mick, get into the seasonal spirit. Featured are (left to right): Phil Horsfall (boxing), Pete White (athletics), Greg Oliver (Pink editor), Michael Austin (rugby), John Lamb (deputy sports editor), Ken Widdows (sports sub-editor), Jim Marshall (horse racing and darts) and Neville Foulger (Coventry City FC reporter).

Getting into the spirit...

There was never much time off over Christmas on the Telegraph so it was imperative to celebrate when possible. Here the tradition is upheld by sports desk stalwarts in the Donkey Box of the Town Wall Tavern, known as the Telegraph's district office.

Pictured (left to right): Steve Evans (who reported on both the Sky Blues and Coventry rugby), Roger Draper (sports editor), Mike Malyon (sports sub-editor and reporter) and Greg Oliver (PINK editor).

Telegraph photographer Bob Cole, who sadly died shortly after supplying several photographs for Telegraph People, took the picture. *There is a tribute to Bob on page 157.*

Marking Cov's 100th year

Front page of a special edition produced by the Telegraph in Corporation Street to celebrate Coventry rugby team's centenary in 1974.

John Lamb edited the special edition and rugby reporter Michael Austin wrote the stories.

The front page shows two "Cov" legends Phil Judd (left) and Ivor Preece. They captained Coventry and England and represented Warwickshire. They were both products of Broadstreet, one of Coventry's most successful rugby clubs.

Fly-half Preece, whose Coventry centre son Peter also represented England in the Seventies, won his 12 caps between 1948 and 1951. Prop Judd, part of a legendary Coventry front row with Mike McLean and Bert Godwin, won 22 England caps between 1963 and 1966

The Pink - 2

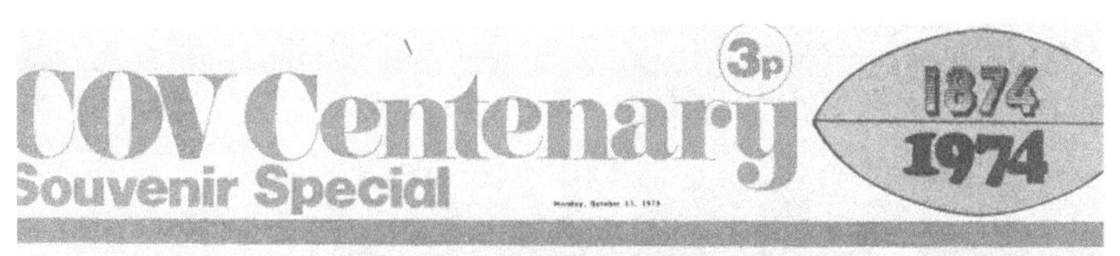

Rugby controversy

John Lamb reported on one of the most controversial matches played at the Coundon Road home of Coventry RFC in October, 1979.

It featured a match between the club and the South African Barbarians at the height of anti-apartheid protests in the UK.

Coundon Road was packed and there was a ring of steel in the shape of West Midlands police outside the ground to keep protesters at bay. This was despite the Barbarians having a multiracial squad.

Lamb, reporting for the Birmingham Mail, met several journalist colleagues in the Town Wall Tavern along with Cov legend David Duckham. They received much abuse on arrival at the ground.

In the picture the Barbarians No 8, Bob Louw, is on his way to an 80-yard try in which he ran through half of the Coventry team and then, as shown here, outpaced the rest. He has even given wing Martin Clifford (right) a head start. The Coventry man could not take advantage and the South Africans won 41-24.

The cutting of Lamb's Sportstalk column about a controversial incident at Coventry Rugby Club's Coundon Road when prop Keith Fairbrother was accused of spitting at a Bridgend spectator. Keith denied the incident and Lamb came to his defence.

Meet Charlie Tustin . .

BEFORE a cloud of vague indifference descends, a word of explanation about the late Charlie Tustin (right).

Charlie was Coventry rugger club's sponge man during the 1920's and 30's and if you had been around at that time, you would have known of him, at least.

For Charlie really was a darlin'. He was the terror of the Coventry dressing-room. One word from him—and you did it.

But he has also left an impression on those at the "Evening Telegraph" who were involved in the production of the Cov Centenary Special.

Of the hundreds of pictures sifted for the special, you could count on Charlie being [illegible] least half—standing with that same haunting glare on the edge of every team group.

. . . and back to present

A time and place for everything

Keith Fairbrother . . . openly hostile to some of his fellow Welsh rugger players.

IT will not have escaped your notice that there is little love lost between Keith Fairbrother and his fellow Welsh rugby players.

Sportstalk . . . with John Lamb

In fact the Coventry prop forward has been known to be openly hostile towards his counterparts from the Principality.

"I hate these bad losing Welshmen" was his most famous observation in a newspaper on the morning of an England-Wales international in which he was participating a few years ago.

Not the most diplomatic statement but Fairbrother must have known what he was letting himself in for. However, his latest brush with a Welshman is not so straightforward.

Neville Walsh, a Bridgend vice-president, claims that the former England player spat at him after the match at Coundon Road on Saturday. Fairbrother says he did not.

Walsh says he admonished Fairbrother for not clapping in the 13 Welshmen (one was sent off, the other staggered off) and was signing autographs instead. Ever tried to clap and write your own name at the same time?

Enjoyment

Walsh says he would have preferred a punch on the nose to the alleged phlegm in the eye. He must therefore feel he deserved something for the remark.

Solicitor Walsh apparently revels in courtroom banter in his home town of Port Talbot. He also appears to enjoy a little contretemps in his favourite pastime of rugger.

As well as firing off complaints to Coventry and the Rugby Football Union, he has requested cuttings of any newspaper stories on the subject. He also refuses to accept Coventry's [illegible]

[illegible] member of London Welsh, member of Saracens, for whom he used to play, vice-chairman of Bridgend tour fund-raising committee.

But his sporting activities do not end at rugger. He is a vice-president of Glamorgan County Cricket Club and was chairman of the Tony Lewis Benefit Fund last season.

The Bridgend supporters at Coundon Road on Saturday were among the most vociferous to visit the ground this season. They obviously wanted their club to beat Coventry and were highly delighted with the 10-10 draw their depleted heroes achieved.

But perhaps the lesson to be learned from Walsh's claim is that you stay well clear of Rugby players still fired up directly after a match.

Any complaints about their ungracious attitude (like not clapping off opponents) should be taken up in the bar later on . . .

CHAPTER 10

Non-PCness in foreign places

These were still heady days, when we were allowed to send reporters abroad to cover events that had a direct impact on our region. We dispatched Alex Goodman to cover the Olympics in West Germany in the summer of 1972. The Games became notorious for the Munich massacre, when Palestinian terrorist group Black September took 11 Israeli team members hostage and killed them along with a West German police officer.

While this act of terror dominated the headlines, there were dramas on the sporting front. The world went wild over a tiny 17-year-old USSR gymnast Olga Korbet for her performance in the team competition on the uneven parallel bars.

I called Alex to tell him what a stir she was causing, with viewers switching on televisions in their millions to watch a sport they had barely heard of.

I don't think Alex had ever seen an uneven parallel bars performance let alone knowing anything about it. However, he did a great job in tracking down the diminutive Belarusian star and filed a cracking story for the *Telegraph*.

Alex also reported on the massacre but the assignment was memorable for him and his colleagues for an incident in the media centre.

He had to be there early in the morning to link up with a copytaker in the Corporation Street offices for the first edition of the *Telegraph* because the paper was printed throughout the day.

He was dictating the intro, which had a phrase about something happening for the first time "since Hitler's 1936 Olympics in Berlin". Unfortunately, the copytaker couldn't grasp the world "Hitler" over the crackly telephone line.

Not matter how many times Alex spelled it out, she simply couldn't hear what he was saying. He was trying to keep his voice down because at that time of the day the media centre was full of journalists reporting for the West and East German press.

However, the red-headed Alex, one of whose virtues was definitely not patience (in fact he used to answer his office telephone by barking YES!), finally snapped. He stood up in the middle of the press room and shouted at the top of his voice "HITLER – FUCKING H-I-T-L-E-R HITLER!".

Many of the West and East German journalists fled for the door until they realised that it was a red-faced man from Coventry barking his orders into a telephone.

Our real interest was in Coventry Godiva athlete Sheila Carey (née Taylor), who finished fifth in the 1500 metres, setting a new British record.

One of our other foreign trips was when Coventry City undertook their maiden voyage into Europe. They finished high enough in the First Division to qualify for the 1970-71 Inter-Cities Fairs Cup along with fellow English clubs Newcastle United, Arsenal, Liverpool and the eventual winners Leeds United.

City's first opponents were the Bulgarian side Trakia Plovdiv and City achieved a 4-1 away win, with a hat-trick from John O'Rourke, followed by a 2-0 home win in the second leg.

We sent Derek Henderson to cover the Wednesday night game on September 16, 1970, in Bulgaria and he needed to file live for a special edition we were publishing by carrying his report in the late news slot.

I was designated to be the copytaker that evening. But we had dreadful trouble trying to make contact with Derek. We kept losing his call but luckily the match was being reported on local radio.

With the help of my colleagues, I was able to cobble a report together but they were not all Derek's words. When I told him he couldn't hide his disappointment on his first major international job and broke down in tears of frustration.

Anyway, we got the special edition out and sold many of them in the pubs and clubs in and around Coventry. Derek was not a happy bunny when he returned to the office but was cheered when City drew Bayern Munich in the next round.

His spirits dropped when City crashed 6-1 at the Grunwalder Stadion in Munich to a Bayern team packed with internationals, including Franz Beckenbauer and Gerd Muller. But at least City did go on to win the second leg 2-1 at Highfield Road on Tuesday, November 3, 1970.

I also remember Derek for a phrase he used when reporting on a major soccer tournament. I don't recall the exact match or country it was played in but Derek wrote something that would be regarded as highly Non-PC today.

He said of an African team competing in the tournament that they regarded "defence as something you sat on". The thought police would quickly delete such a phrase today.

German tour

Our man (Derek Henderson or NEMO as he was previously called) is pictured kneeling far right with manager Jimmy Hill (centre) and Coventry City players at the start of a close-season tour of West Germany in May, 1962.

Back row: Unknown West German official; Frank Kletzenbauer; Brian Hill; Colin Holder; Albert McCann; George Curtis; Stuart Imlach; Peter Hill; Roy Dwight; Frank Austin; John Sillett; Ron Farmer; Arthur Lightening.

Front row: Dietmar Bruck; Bob Wesson; manager Jimmy Hill; Unknown German official; Derek Henderson (NEMO).

It was at the end of Hill's first season at Highfield Road when the Sky Blues (Derek was credited with creating the phrase) finished 14th in the Third Division.

The West German officials were entertaining the party for a three-match tour against Hanau 1893 (won 3-2 with two goals from Farmer and a penalty from Imlach), Hassfurt 1917 (won 2-0 with Farmer and Imlach goals) and Singen 1904 (won 3-0 through a goal from Brian Hill and two from John Sillett, who with George Curtis led City to FA Cup glory against Tottenham Hotspur in 1987).

Colin Holder and Coventry City Former Players' Association

Record crowd at Cov's home

The record crowd at Coundon Road, believed to be the County Championship final between Warwickshire and Lancashire in 1963. Warwickshire won 8-6 during a period when they dominated the Championship. The picture was captured from the roof of the clubhouse by Ernie Askill, who was working for the weekly Coventry Standard at the time. He eventually became picture editor on the Telegraph. The mounted picture, found under the main stand at Coundon Road, is severely water-damaged.

CHAPTER 11

Foreign labour

We always seemed to be on the lookout for journalists in the Seventies. In fact we came to believe that if anyone wandered in off the streets saying they were semi-literate and were looking for a job they would be taken on immediately. And that is exactly what happened. An American guy whose name I only remember as Maurice called into the front office and announced to the receptionist that he was a journalist and was looking for work.

I don't know who went to see him but he was working on the news sub-editors' desk the next day. It turned out, when we quizzed him over a few beers in the Town Wall, that the bearded Maurice was touring the world in an attempt to dodge the draft to Vietnam, where America had been waging a war since 1965.

We were all pretty much opposed to US operations in the Far East and Maurice did not want to become one of the 58,220 US troops who were victims of that ill-advised conflict. So he was welcomed into our fold.

He got on well with everyone except, sadly, his bosses. He was trying to fit in with the English way of journalism and the language. But his days on news ended when he was given a court story to edit which involved a handler of stolen goods being jailed.

Maurice's headline was: **FENCE GETS TERM BEHIND BARS**. We thought this amusing and would have been fine in the *New York Times*. But it did not go down well with his superiors, who were looking for a far more English approach to headline writing.

So Maurice was moved to the features desk but only to achieve similar results. So for some reason senior management were reluctant to part with Maurice and decided his future lay with the sports desk. Goodness knows why because he knew less about British sport than he did about our judicial system.

We didn't really know what to do with him. And we immediately had him down as a brain box because he whiled away the hours of inactivity learning Greek from a French book.

It turned out that Maurice had arrived from Greece, where he claimed he had been engaged as a proof reader by a publishing company. We never established exactly what the publication was and we felt reluctant to disturb him from his studies.

At the time, we were giving heavy coverage to the 1968 Olympics in Mexico City. These were the Olympics that became infamous if not notorious for the action of two black American athletes Tommie Smith and John Carlos, who had finished first and third respectively in the 200 metres.

When they stood on the podium to receive their medals they gave black-gloved fist salutes as a "mark of solidarity with the oppressed" during the American national anthem.

The Games were also famous for the high jumper Dick Fosbury, who won the gold medal using what was then a revolutionary technique to clear the barrier by gliding over it backwards, with his belly uppermost. It became known as the Fosbury Flop and is the technique used exclusively by today's high jumpers.

The Games were also notable for long-jumper Bob Beamon, who recorded a phenomenal leap of 8.90 metres (29ft 2in). The *Telegraph* in those days was pioneering colour-printing techniques at their Corporation Street plant and was the first daily newspaper to print a colour picture of Beamon's remarkable feat.

However, it was none of these epoch-making incidents, that made the Games memorable for me. Maurice the American did it. It was my turn to do the early Olympics pages and the first routine every morning was to send out several stories we called fillers.

These tiny stories of up to three paragraphs were invaluable for filling gaps when the pages were made up in metal. I gave Maurice about half-a-dozen small stories like this to edit while I got on with planning the pages.

It wasn't until I was given a proof that I noticed one of Maurice's fillers had been used at the bottom of the page. It was only one paragraph and the headline he had written on the cycling story was: **PEDAL MEDAL**.

I have never forgotten Maurice for that small gem and shortly afterwards he left for somewhere in Europe, never to be heard of again. We also felt it was rather odd for a man who didn't want to go to war to habitually wear denim combat gear.

Our other foreign colleague was an Aussie called Frazer Guild. He was a total cricket fanatic who never worked on the sports desk. But he certainly made an impression on us.

He was a news sub and in his half-hour lunch break would often head for the Woolworth store in the city centre. He wasn't interested in any of the goods sold there. It was the security cameras that held more intrigue.

Frazer was not involved in petty pilfering. He used the security cameras, which monitored activity in the shopping aisles, to check his bowling action. He would tear up and down dodging genuine shoppers to check on the screen that his action was legal. He was convinced he was "a chucker" and often dragged one of us along to check him out.

We assured him all was well and he did make the *Telegraph* cricket team. He decided to return to Australia and a long thrash in the Town Wall Tavern was organised. Frazer became a little worse for wear and returned to the office. He slumped into one of the sports desk seats and promptly threw up over the typewriter in front of him.

Bits of tomato skin and carrot would fly out of the machine for months afterwards whenever anyone tried to write a story on it. Frazer headed back to Oz and we did receive a letter from him saying that on the way home he had achieved a life-long ambition.

He stopped off at Lord's cricket ground in London and was able to peer through the railings and look at the wicket at the home of cricket. "My life is now complete," he wrote in a postcard, never to be heard of again.

The 'branch office'...

The Town Wall Tavern public house behind the Belgrade Theatre, pictured as it looks today, was a favourite haunt of Telegraph editorial staff. Its famous Donkey Box (second door from the left) was hired one Christmas by Telegraph sports personnel Roger Draper and Greg Oliver, replete in black ties and dinner suits, for a sumptuous lunch prepared by landlord Ray Hoare's wife with Ray acting as a suitably-dressed waiter. Occasionally there would be an attempt to break the record of getting as many people as possible into the tiny room.

The Coventry Evening Telegraph Golf Society prepare for action at the Hill Valley Golf and Country Club in Shropshire. Sky Blues reporter Neville Foulger, who succeeded Derek Henderson, is second left on the back row with photographer Bob Cole sitting bottom right.

CHAPTER 12

Lunch-time trysts and promotion

On Merv's departure, Derek Henderson, the Chief Football Writer, was appointed sports editor. This enraged No 2 Tony Lanigan because Derek had no production experience and little interest in any sports other than soccer. Tony left to join the *Daily Mail* in Manchester and his move was a great success.

The affable Brian Payne was appointed deputy and life settled into a pleasant and ever-changing atmosphere. But there was a huge shock from Derek "Mr Sky Blues" Henderson, who decided to move to his native Wolverhampton on the *Express* and *Star*. He would then move to Cornwall before going back to the Midlands and joining me on my first day at the *Birmingham Evening Mail*, much to my surprise.

Brian had also moved on and this meant that Alan Parr was appointed sports editor and he named me as his deputy, much to the surprise of Ken Widdows, who fully expected to get the No 2 job from his good friend Alan.

It all went pretty smoothly but Ken's reputation for a casual approach to the job, which probably cost him the No 2 spot, continued.

His time-keeping was erratic and on one occasion failed to file a report of a Friday night Nuneaton Borough match in time for the first Saturday edition after over-doing the post-match drinks. This caused us to rapidly fill the space with a fairly meaningless story for the first edition.

Anyway, Ken, a very competent operator when he was at his desk, survived in part because of his close association with the *Telegraph's* cricket team, in which one of the leading players was managing director Tim Morris.

I couldn't really argue because the bar largely funded the cricket team, also supported by editor Keith Whetstone, who had succeeded John Leese. It was during this time that the *Telegraph* decided to create a large editorial floor occupied by most of the journalists. So the walls between the sub-editors' office and the old sports room and a few management offices were demolished.

This opened up the whole floor and the reporters joined us from a separate room. The sports desk was moved from a location overlooking Belgrade Square to one with a view of the rectangle with a monumental pond around which the offices were built.

And it was on to this floor that a new tea trolley lady rattled on her first morning. However, she did not last long. She went back to her base in the canteen and told her boss that she would not be staying in a company where the people she was serving were so rude and their language appalling.

Asked to explain, she said that when she arrived in the sub-editors' department, they simply sat there and shouted at her: "COFFEE, FUCKING COFFEE, OVER HERE, NOW!"

The new lady decided to stay on only after it was explained to her that the journalists were not shouting COFFEE! but COPY! urging the copy boys and girls to get their edited material into the composing room for setting in type.

There were many incidents and one involved a gentleman who was known throughout the office as Mr Loony. He had stalked a few reporters in an issue over something that he been written about him.

He eventually turned his vitriol on editor Geoff Elliott. It all came to a head one lunchtime when I noticed movement on the roof of the build overlooking the rectangle around which the offices were built.

There was a figure standing on the edge three storeys up and it turned out to be Mr Loony.

After alerting a photographer and then the police, Geoff and I ran to a window overlooking where he was standing. We urged him to get on with it if he was going to jump because we had a newspaper to get out and we would want a picture of him heading for the ornamental pond below.

Our bluff worked and he was eventually carried away by the police. I'm not sure what the conclusion of this unhappy episode was but I doubt this experience was enough to deter Mr Loony from his crazy ways.

After about 10 years on the sport desk, during which time my children Joanne and James had been born in 1973 and 1976 respectively, it was time to move on.

Towards the end of the decade, I was approached by the *Birmingham Evening Mail*, an Iliffe Group sister paper, about joining them as chief sports sub-editor. The *Mail* had a vastly bigger circulation – in those days nudging half-a-million – and, more importantly, higher salaries.

It also covered an area that included six top football clubs. I was asked to introduce rugby coverage to the Sports Argus – the *Mail's* equivalent to the *PINK* – marking a huge departure given that most Brummies had never seen the game played with an oval-shaped ball.

They were offering me £2,000 a year more than the *Telegraph* were paying me. I was in a quandary because I was quite happy at the *Telegraph* but was tempted by a huge rise at the time.

Editor Keith said he would not match the money so I gave in my notice and then in 1977 started the daily trek into the Mail's Colmore Circus headquarters in central Birmingham.

The scribe of Highfield Road

Derek Henderson, who at one time was NEMO, bids farewell to Coventry City's Highfield Road in 1973 after covering the club for 15 years. He was a consummate sports reporter and had total impartiality, even though he was devoted to the club. He coined the nickname Sky Blues when City played Birmingham City in a pre-season friendly before their debut in the First Division. Their kit, for the first time, included Sky Blue shirts. Ironically, the City were playing their "home" matches at the Blues' St Andrew's stadium in the 2019-20 season during disputes over use of the Ricoh Arena.

Photographers on the razzle

Photographers let their hair down on a night out at the Two Boats public house in Long Itchington. Dennis Morgan, who sadly died this year, is the centre of attention.

CHAPTER 13

...Birmingham and London

For the sake of continuity, I feel I should devote a chapter to my time between visits No 2 and No 3 to the *Telegraph* in Corporation Street. It was a hugely significant time for me but not directly relevant to the *Telegraph*.

However, I learned so many lessons on the *Birmingham Evening Mail* and the *London Evening News* that I was able to bring much experience and expertise back to the *Telegraph* when I returned in 1980.

I arrived at the *Birmingham Mail* on Monday, September 12, 1977, to start my duties as chief sports sub-editor. It was a long trek compared to the *Telegraph* and involved a walk to the Canley station a mile from my home in Coventry, a train into New Street Station, Birmingham, and a walk across the city centre to Colmore Circus.

My journey was eased on occasion by Tony Dickens, who worked on the *Mail* news desk and rose to become its deputy editor.

He would travel by car on the A45 to get from his outpost in far-flung Stretton-on-Dunsmore into central Birmingham and would pass within a quarter of mile of my house in Coventry at an extremely early hour.

He would pick me up near the junction with Broad Lane – when he remembered that is. He once drove straight past me, leaving me stranded in a horizontal blizzard.

The *Mail* newsroom was enormous compared with the *Telegraph* and housed not only the *Mail* journalists but those on the daily *Birmingham Post*, the weekly *Sports Argus* and the *Sunday Mercury*.

My 7.30 start that first morning was distinguished by unexpectedly bumping into Derek Henderson, who was joining the *Argus* as a soccer reporter and controversial columnist. Sadly, Derek was never going to be the sort of controversial columnist who would provoke anger and indignation among the fans.

Another shock awaited me. A few weeks later a former *Telegraph* sports desk colleague, Pete White, turned up at the *Mail* to join *Sports Argus* editor Ian Johnson.

Pete and I had our moments on the *Telegraph*, nearly coming to blows on one occasion.

As well as the two major clubs, Aston Villa and Birmingham City, the coverage area of the papers included West Bromwich Albion, Wolverhampton Wanderers, Coventry City and Walsall.

My bosses were Brian Sparkes, the sports editor, and Vic Wakeling, his deputy. The ultimate boss, and the one who had hired me, was Leon Hickman, assistant editor, sports.

Leon was not well liked by the staff and, of course, I guess in turn they were prepared not to like me because I was "his man".

However, I got on great once I had proved to my new colleagues that I knew what I was doing. This was a much bigger operation and my main role was to turn the pages designed by Brian and Vic into reality, or at least hot metal.

I used to work Monday to Friday so that I could cover a rugby match on Saturdays in the winter. But this was a very flimsy arrangement and was often changed due to staff shortages in the office on the *Argus*.

Saturday was a long day, starting with the London edition. The *Evening News* and the *Standard* in London had stopped publishing on Saturdays so the *Mail* tried to fill the gap by rushing an early edition to the capital.

Then there were editions of the white followed by two of the *Argus*. Some of my colleagues would then go on to work on the *Mercury* for extra money but I never took advantage, preferring to have a night out.

I hugely enjoyed my time on the *Mail*. Life was much stricter than on the *Telegraph*, with "Sparky" controlling our hours, especially at lunch-time. Half-an-hour was permitted, enabling us to grab a pint or two in the Queen's Head over the road if you ate at your desk to save time.

You were paid extra for starting work half-an-hour earlier, taking only a half-hour lunch and staying on an extra half-hour over and above the hours agreed by the National Union of Journalists.

When Vic Wakeling, who I had grown to respect massively, accepted a job on the *London Evening News* Sports Desk, I was offered the role of assistant sports editor.

This meant occasionally stepping into Sparky's role, whose habit was to take Fridays off, the second busiest day of the week. So I took control of the back page, a frenetic operation with most of our leading clubs announcing teams for the next day's matches.

Brian, although diligent and hard working, simply wanted to retire as early as possible. I'm not sure why but he had a particular liking for Canada and wanted to retire there.

He was also notorious for exaggerating. He once announced that Jack Hobbs was dead when the Australian cricket legend was ill. A quick flash was written for the late news and we only just stopped it when the truth became apparent.

He once told me his house was flooded and when I commiserated with Mrs Sparkes when I answered his phone, she said: "What's he talking about – a tap's leaking."

He also announced that Mrs. Sparkes was very ill, having contracted brucellosis, which was prevalent among cattle at the time. Mrs S, I'm glad to report, had a heavy cold.

Brian used to plan all of his pages for every edition through the whole week in advance and store his "charts", as he called them, in his bottom drawer.

I preferred a more instantaneous routine and left my back page design until the latest minute, having primed all the subs on what stories I wanted them to edit.

On my first Friday in charge, one of my duties was to attend early morning conference in the board room to go through our schedule with the editor, David Hopkinson, and other senior colleagues.

I proceeded through my list of stories but became alarmed that I was boring everyone when David picked up the *Financial Times* and opened it up. I had arrived at a cricket item and it was later explained to me that David had no interest in the sport and made it obvious by doing something else.

Then one Friday, Ray Matts, the chief football writer who went on to cover the Midlands and motor sport for the *Daily Mail*, sidled over and slipped a piece of paper with a phone number on my desk and whispered to give Vic a ring.

I duly did as bid and Vic Wakeling asked if I'd like to join him as deputy sports editor of the *London Evening News*. I had only been at the *Mail* for two years but was tempted and Ann and I travelled to London for a chat.

We met in the Tipperary pub off a teeming Fleet Street. I was immediately captivated and accepted the job. No more formality was necessary in those days and I joined the *Daily Mail* stable-mate in October, 1979.

Vic introduced me to my new colleagues and, again, I detected a frisson of resentment, which I understood because at least two of them had aspired to the job Vic had given me.

One of my new colleagues was the legendary Reg Gutteridge, who was the boxing reporter and second only to the BBC's Harry Carpenter because he also worked for ITV.

"I 'ate Brummies," Reg said as we shook hands. After explaining I was from Coventry, Reg apologised. When I asked why he hated Brummies, he explained that he had been injured during the Dunkirk evacuation in the Second World War and his leg had to be amputated – in Birmingham.

"They've still got my leg," he complained. Reg became a great friend of Mohammed Ali, who he shocked at the dinner table one night in the States by plunging his knife into his own wooden leg. I'm not sure why, but I guess it seemed a good idea at the time and Reg wanted a bit of attention.

Reg was also well known on US television and when a host said he understood he had lost his leg in the war, Reg replied: "Yeh, why you found it?"

Fleet Street was full of legends like Reg. In fact our "local", the Harrow, had a bar dedicated to one of our *Daily Mail* colleagues, Vincent Mulchrone, who could write like an angel especially after one or two "attitude adjusters" in the Champagne Bar.

He would apparently enter his own Vincent Mulchrone Champagne bar and loudly exclaim: "Landlord, flood the bar with your finest Champagne."

After a week, Vic took his first holiday for about a year, leaving me in charge and giving me an opportunity to earn my spurs.

On my first day in charge I arrived extra early in order to get the pages into shape and read every sports page in the mornings to ensure that we were on top of everything.

The department heads were required to take their schedules for the day to the editor's office for morning conference. I had a good schedule and entered the hallowed ground confidently.

The news editor, Charles Garside, went first followed by me. After going through my meticulous list, Louis asked: "What about the Charlie George story?"

I wracked my brains but could recall no mention of the Arsenal star in the mornings. Charles, who was to become a life-long if not frequent friend, saved my bacon when he told Louis it was a news story and he was on to it.

When we exited Charlie told me he also hadn't a clue what Louis was talking about. However, close examination of the *Daily Mail* gossip column by Nigel Dempster, revealed a one-paragraph footnote alleging Charlie George had been ejected from a London club for being drunk.

I never missed reading the Dempster footnote again.

I had been staying in the Y-hotel (as in YMCA) in Tottenham Court Road, having used the influence of a friend's friend to become a permanent resident there. There was a long waiting list for the small but perfectly fine rooms but I managed to leap the queue.

I stayed there until Charles generously allowed me to move in with him and his then girlfriend Carole, in Trinity Church Square, Southwark, rent free.

Charles became a good friend and in later years I worked with him on the *Evening Standard*. He was a consummate journalist – one of the best I ever worked with.

We used to start work at silly o'clock on the *News* and the deal was that I had to get up first to use the shower. This led to my only spat with him. He had been out fishing one night and left a slimy mess of what I think was trout in the bath. I quickly discovered this to my alarm when I tried to take a shower at that early hour.

But life was pretty good. A great job, a young family and all the social trappings which went with being in Fleet Street. Then a bombshell...

Having a laugh...

John Lamb and Keith Dovkants (right), then chief reporter of the London Evening Standard, share a light moment in the newsroom. Keith, a great all-rounder, filed one of the first Standard stories by digital technology when he covered the riots in Tiananmen Square in Beijing in 1989.

Standard Shenanigans

Comedy actress Cleo Rocos joins in the fun as journalists from the London Evening Standard, including John Lamb, enjoy themselves while raising money to help buy St Thomas's Hospital in London a scanner. Cleo, also a producer, presenter and businesswoman who starred with Kenny Everett in the TV show The Kenny Everett Television, was happy to throw herself into pulling in a charity tug-of-war contest held just off Oxford Street. Pictured are (left to right): Andy Bordiss, John Lamb, Charles Garside. David Meilton, Cleo, hidden unknown, Dick Murray and Shekhar Bhatia. Bob Graham is on his knees.

STANDARD
SCANNER
APPEAL
AWAY

News room

Down to business: The Evening Standard news room winds down at the end of the day while John Lamb goes through the next day's diary with reporters.

This shows the legendary Standard newsroom in the Daily Express's Fleet Street headquarters, known as the Black Lubyanka after the Moscow secret services headquarters. The listed building, clad in black Vitrolite panels with chromium strips at the joints, had a magnificent art deco reception.

But upstairs was a different story as can be witnessed in the picture. Even with all of its imperfections it was a great place to work, says Lamb.

FIRE EXIT

A warm welcome...

Vic Wakeling, sports editor of the Evening News in London, offers a warm welcome to John Lamb as his deputy. John, who had worked with Vic on the Birmingham Evening Mail, always rated the Geordie as one of the best journalists he worked with. After the closure of the Evening News, Vic went into television and became the boss of Sky Sports, where his position was virtually ring-fenced by owner Rupert Murdoch. Vic died in 2018.

Evening News

TELEPHONE: 01-353 6000
TELEGRAMS: EVENINGNEWS, LONDON-E.C.4

REGISTERED OFFICE
CARMELITE HOUSE,
LONDON, EC4Y OJA
REGISTERED NO. 1160345 ENGLAND

John Lamb Esq
3 Coral Close
(off Broad Lane)
COVENTRY

12 October 1979

Dear John,

Just a line to say a personal welcome to the Evening News. I am sure that we'll enjoy working together.

Nadia is sending you copies of all our editions, and I would welcome any ideas or thoughts you may have. When you are settled in, I shall be hoping that we can tidy up the appearance of the sports pages.

In the meantime, milk all your Midland associates for rugby contacts in the south, and if there is anything I can do to help you personally in your move, please let me know.

Yours sincerely

Vic Wakeling

Vic Wakeling

CHAPTER 14

A bombshell...then back to Corporation St.

I moved the family south, settling into a lovely detached house with dormer windows but this was in Hullbridge, near Rayleigh in Essex. I moved there against all the best advice, which said I should buy a flat in London and a house on the coast, possibly Brighton. The Hullbridge area seemed to be full of tattoo-clad London gangsters keeping their heads down while driving around in Rolls-Royces.

Then came the unwelcome news. It was announced on my birthday, October 1, 1980, that the *Evening News* was to close at the end of the month.

The paper, which had been the favourite of East Enders for many years, had lost its survival battle with the *Evening Standard*, which had a much smaller circulation but was a bigger attraction for up-market advertisers.

The *Evening News* had tried to go up-market to challenge the *Standard* but it was too late and so the adrenalin of having two evening papers in the same city competing fiercely ended for us.

On some days, we would receive the first edition of the *Standard* and like their back page lead story so much that we would substantiate it and swop it with our lead. They would often do the same.

We should have known something was up because only a few months earlier, editor Louis Kirby had invited his "top executives" to a dinner at the swanky Stafford Hotel in St James. It was a three-line whip.

We gathered on the evening of Friday, February 1, 1980, to have "in a relaxed atmosphere", a close look at the objectives of the *Evening*

News in the 1980's (sic) and to stimulate a useful dialogue about our approach to the job in the future.

"The editor asks you to consider: Are there things we should be doing and don't? Are there things we are doing and shouldn't?".

"I think we can expect a lively, informative and entertaining evening."

Over a sumptuous meal, we had a wide-ranging discussion and we were assured that the *Evening News* was thriving.

I note now that the portents were not good. There were 13 people around that table. Exactly nine months later – on Friday, October 1 – it was announced that the *News* would close.

The last edition was on Friday, October 31, 1980, and we published just one edition with **GOODBYE LONDON** as the splash headline.

The sports desk marked the occasion in the office wake by sending a taxi down the Old Kent Road for about 15 portions of the apocryphal pie, mash and liquor (cabbage water) with jellied eels on the top for everyone.

On top of the alcohol, we felt as if we had eaten a brick. No wonder East End urchins could keep running for days on this sort of fodder.

John Leese, my former editor from Coventry, was given the unenviable task of taking charge of the paper while it went through its valedictory month.

The *Evening News* title had been sold to the *Express* Group, owners of the *Standard*, for a nominal £1 and Louis Kirby left the sinking ship to become the editor of our former evening rival.

After the euphoria of the party had died down, I started arranging shifts on other Fleet Street papers. They were generous and I did stints mainly on the Daily and Sunday *Mirror*.

The trouble was you spent most of the evening in the pub – in this case the White Hart. This hostelry was known throughout Fleet Street as The Stab – where you went to stab your colleagues in the back.

You also spent most of your shift money – in the bar. After popping back to edit a couple of stories, I then had the extreme discomfort of trying to survive the Tube and train journey back to Rayleigh in carriages with no toilet.

Relief came when I was offered Saturday afternoon shifts on the *News of the World* sports desk and after a few weeks they made me a "permanent casual", working on Thursday, Friday and Saturday, entitling me to holiday pay, which was amazing.

The pay was generous at £120 a shift – in cash – and meant that I could get by. I seem to remember we were given £6,000 by Associated Newspaper Group, owner of the *Mail* and *News*, as a redundancy payment, which also helped.

I also received a rise when the *News of World* discovered I could handle pictures and write decent captions.

Legendary sports editor Frank Butler had taken me for a beer to tell me about the rise. We sat at the bar of the Tipperary and Frank suddenly said in a broad Cockney accent: " 'ere, you know that Adolf 'itler?"

I said – while rather bemused making a rather obvious answer to the question, – that I did. Frank, who at 24 had become the youngest sports editor in Fleet Street when he joined the *Daily Express*, said:

"'e used to time all of his most important speeches on a Saturday so that he could catch the first edition of the *News of the World*".

I'm not sure how true that was but, like all good newspapermen and women, he would not let the facts spoil a good story in the pub.

It was a permanent job I wanted but they were rare in Fleet Street, given the number of candidates available because of the *News* closure.

Vic Wakeling obviously made the right decision by going into TV and went on to work for Television South in Southampton. He was to become the head of Sky Sports and was such a success that his job was virtually ring-fenced by Rupert Murdoch, the owner. Sadly, Vic died in 2018.

My thoughts went back to the *Telegraph* because Keith Whetstone had been appointed editor of the *Birmingham Mail*. He was to be succeeded by Geoff Elliott, who I had known from my days as a copy boy and being on the same NCTJ course in Birmingham. He seemed destined to become the *Telegraph* editor and had joined the *Kentish Times* group to cut his teeth in the chair.

We met at his office to talk about the possibility of my joining him and after going through interviews with 11 internal candidates back in Coventry, he offered me the job of assistant editor.

So, it was back to Coventry and Corporation Street, leaving Fleet Street and my family behind.

We should have known better...

Evening News editor Louis Kirby's letter to Lamb and his fellow "top executives" inviting them to a swanky dinner in a Mayfair hotel on January 28, 1980. He assured everyone the paper had a great future. It closed on October 31, 1980, and Lamb returned to the Telegraph.

Evening News

CARMELITE HOUSE
LONDON, EC4Y

28th January, 1980

Dear John

Louis is holding a dinner for top executives at the Stafford Hotel, St. James', on Friday, 1st February.

Will you please make sure you are free to attend.

The main idea of the evening is to have, in a relaxed atmosphere, a close look at the objectives of the Evening News in the 1980's and to stimulate a useful dialogue about our approach to the job in the future.

The editor asks you to consider: Are there things we should be doing and don't? Are there things we are doing and shouldn't?

I think we can expect a lively, informative and entertaining evening.

6.30 for 7.00 start.

Goodbye London and back to Corporation Street

The Evening News staff gather outside the offices they shared with the Daily Mail off Fleet Street. 'Lamb is in there somewhere (near the one-way sign, he thinks)

The Evening News became the centre of the news itself and for the wake Lamb and his colleagues organised lunch by dispatching a cab to the Old Kent Road to buy 15 portions of the East Enders' favourite pie, mash and liquor (cabbage water) with jellied eels on the top.

Only one edition was produced that day with the front page splash headline saying simply: Goodbye London. But news editor Charles Garside told the many media people marking the closure that if a plane came down on Oxford Street, another edition would be produced.

CLOSING

Hello and farewell...

The letter ending John Lamb's employment on the Evening News. It was from John Leese, who had been appointed editor for the final month of the paper's life after the announcement of its closure on October 1,1980. Ironically, Leese had given Lamb his first job as a journalist on the Coventry Evening Telegraph when he was editor there.

Evening News

TELEPHONE: 01-353 6000
TELEGRAPH: EVENINGNEWS, LONDON-EC4

REGISTERED OFFICE
CARMELITE HOUSE,
LONDON, EC4Y OJA
REGISTERED NO. 160545 ENGLAND

October 24, 1980

Dear Mr. Lamb

The last issue of the Evening News will be published next Friday, and it is my sad duty to tell you that the Company has no alternative but to end your employment on October 31, 1980.

Everyone will be paid in the normal way until then, and the starting date for calculating money in lieu of notice will be November 1, 1980.

There will not be time before October 31 to calculate and prepare your full settlements, so on your final pay day this month you will receive an advance on account of your redundancy compensation. This should tide you over until the balance is available.

Before the end of November we will tell you the amount of money due, and the arrangements for paying it. If you have any queries we will do everything we can to help and advise.

Finally, on behalf of the Company, I must thank you for all your efforts for the Evening News, and say how sorry I am that they were unavailing. You have much to take pride in. Good luck and good wishes.

Yours sincerely

John Leese

John Leese
Editor

CHAPTER 15

Adjusting attitudes...

So I returned to Corporation Street in my role as assistant editor. Someone once asked what was the difference between an assistant editor and a deputy editor, and I said: "About two grand a year." I was in effect Geoff's deputy. But that title was held by John Cross, who had been at the *Telegraph* for ever.

He was far happier doing admin stuff and signing the expenses than being a journalist. This point was proved in some of the newspapers Geoff had sent me in advance in order to get a flavour of what the *Telegraph* was like.

Among the bundle was the one that reported John Lennon being shot dead outside the entrance to the Dakota Building overlooking Central Park in New York.

It had happened just before 11pm local time on Monday, December 8, 1980 – 4am on December 9 in Britain. It was a gift for the evening papers then but would be of no value now because the *Telegraph* is published overnight.

Across the UK, editors were tearing up their planned front pages and splashing the headline **LENNON SHOT DEAD** across the top of the front page.

Not at the *Coventry Evening Telegraph*, edited at the time by "Crossie" because Keith had left and Geoff hadn't arrived.

They had a very weak headline that said something about "Ex-Beatle is killed" among a mixture of other news. It was the only story people wanted to read about but there was no clearing of the front page in Coventry.

However, they did carry a small tribute to Lennon on an inside page, again buried among other news stories. The front page cross-reference to the tribute read: "The day the music died," using words from the Don McLean hit. They couldn't even find words by Lennon to use in the headline.

So, the *Telegraph* didn't perform terribly well on that day and I was looking forward to introducing changes at the *CET*.

There were several silly rules that I immediately scrapped. One was a ban from the *CET* columns of *The Specials*, the 2-Tone and ska revival band that had a string of hits from 1979. Their song *Ghost Town* spent three weeks at No 1 and was hailed generally as a biting commentary on urban decay, unemployment and violence in inner cities.

But again not at the *CET* in Corporation Street. The *Coventry Telegraph* upper echelon apparently thought this was about their city (it certainly rang true), took it personally and banned *The Specials* from their columns.

The decision was immediately reversed when Geoff and I arrived and was greeted warmly by the reporters and sub-editors.

Other rulings of a similar kind were uncovered over the months. It followed the same sort of real "old fart" journalism that I later discovered prevailed on the *Telegraph* stable-mate *The Birmingham Post*.

When I was deputy editor on the *Post* some years later I discovered on my first night as duty editor that the subject of AIDS was banned from the front page of the paper.

This emerged when I wanted the death of Chariots of Fire actor Ian Charleson reported across the top of the front page. He had died at 40 after suffering complications from HIV in January, 1990.

I was then informed about the ban but reversed it immediately. I can only imagine that the rule had been imposed by a former, ageing male management who didn't like to admit and openly report a problem among males.

Back at the *Telegraph*, I hoped my experiences on the *Birmingham Evening Mail* and the *London Evening News* would result in an improvement in its content and appearance.

I was flattered to learn that on my first day I had been expected for "lunch" at the Town Wall Tavern by landlord Ray Hoare. He had put John Lamb's Hotpot on the menu in my honour but I skipped lunch. I put my absence right the next day.

Ray, also boss of the local Licensed Victuallers' Association, ran his pub with a fist of iron and didn't suffer fools gladly. Several customers felt the lash of his tongue and were banned for wearing football scarves.

Other victims of Ray's eccentric behaviour were students. He hated them ("they buy nothing, make a noise and smell," he used to say) and he placed a sign over the exit door from the pub that said STUDENTS' ENTRANCE.

The pub attracted all sorts of waifs and strays and one habitué was an actor who turned up to appear in something at the nearby Belgrade Theatre and never left. He was reported to be Stephen Hancock, who played Ernie Bishop in Coronation Street.

That reminds me of a huge embarrassment for me at the Belgrade Theatre when jazzman Humphrey Lyttelton was appearing with his band. I was in the audience and, tipped off by the mischievous Ray, Humph announced to the audience at the end of the performance: "I'm instructed to tell John Lamb that the bar is being kept open late for him at the Town Wall Tavern."

It was, indeed, and Humph was in there to share the joke.

But generally the Town Wall, still a great pub today, was loved by *Telegraph* people for its excellent company, good beer and splendid food prepared by Mrs Hoare.

Every large newspaper I worked for had a "Crossie", a journalist who was far happier doing the admin work than getting involved in the cut and thrust of the day.

He was a perfect character for this task. He was known to be tight-fisted and would make his own, heavy tweed suits that made me itch just to look at them. I was told that he also made his own shoes.

He was no happier than when he was slashing reporters' expenses. He would dutifully take a tape measure to a map to check the mileage, which, of course, was always far less than the reporters' estimates. After his calculations, reporters began to feel that places like Warwick Crown Court were getting closer to the office.

One of my first "rude awakening" moments on my return was on a Saturday afternoon when I was not on duty. This was Saturday, June 13, 1981, when shots were fired at the Queen as she rode down The Mall to the Trooping of the Colour ceremony.

The shots turned out to be blanks but the media went berserk – except the unflappable *Coventry Evening Telegraph*. The incident had happened at 2.48pm, giving plenty of time. Even though they could have re-plated the front page and produced a Late Night Final edition, they didn't.

To be fair, a normal Late Night Final was not usually published on Saturdays because the *PINK* was coming out later. But the *Telegraph* sat on its collective fingers after receiving a flash in red from the Press Association.

I didn't find out about the incident until I returned home too late (no mobile telephones in those days to get breaking news). So I thought it wise to have a small inquest on the Monday morning. I was told that after the Press Association (PA) flash, news of the incident dried up and there were no further details.

No-one on the staff thought of calling PA to find out what was going on (as many other newspapers did). A story could easily have been rushed together with a couple of paragraphs on the incident and then perhaps 100 words about Trooping of the Colour. A headline **SHOTS FIRED AT QUEEN** might have captured the attention.

But not even a television was switched on and not a thought was given to running a story in the *PINK*. It could have occupied a single column alongside the sports reports.

To be fair to the staff at the *Telegraph*, this was the mindset that had developed over many years of inertia. I also detected that there was a sort anti-royal sentiment among the younger staff.

I quickly tried to disabuse them of this because I pointed out that, no matter what their feelings, the Royals subliminally (and not) sold millions of newspapers around the world so they should really love them for helping to keep them in employment.

I had learned in my earlier days on the *Telegraph* that circulation increased substantially when you put a Royal picture on the front page, especially in colour.

The *Telegraph* had led the field in being able to publish same-day colour pictures, as they did of Bob Beamon's monstrous long jump at the 1968 Mexico Olympics.

I'm not sure my words about the Royals had much impact but I was determined we would give the Royal Wedding to end all Royal Weddings between Prince Charles and Lady Diana Spencer proper treatment.

It was my routine to check early every morning with my former colleagues on the *Evening News* who now worked on the *Standard* what was really going on.

I spoke to my old drinking buddy and colleague Aldo Nicolotti on the news desk and he told me there was to be an announcement from Buckingham Palace at 11am that Prince Charles and Lady Diana Spencer were to confirm their engagement.

Unsurprisingly, we didn't have a clue but the early tip allowed us to set up a front page lead on the engagement story and get a load of background for the inside pages. We simply had to wait for the live pictures.

So we were able to sell many extra copies of the Lunch Edition with a bill on the streets, which said something like: "Prince Charles to wed". Who could resist buying a copy even if they would have a *Telegraph* delivered to their home later?

We were breaking news in a way that would be impossible today because social media now always gets in first.

I made meticulous plans for the wedding on Wednesday, July 29, 1981, which was declared a national holiday. I negotiated with the Newspaper Society for the *Telegraph* to have both a photographer's and reporter's position in St Paul's, where the wedding was to take place.

In those pre-digital days it also meant engaging a DR (dispatch rider) to bring films back from central London. As well as reporting the ceremony on the day (watched by 750 million people on TV worldwide but not by most of the *Telegraph* reporters, I suspected), we produced a colour supplement the following day.

It attracted much acclaim and the front page carried the famous picture of the happy couple kissing on the balcony at Buckingham Palace. Not the work of our own man but his material was used widely on the inside pages.

And I hope I won over some of the journalists as to the value of Royal stories, even the raving republicans.

One of my colleagues at this time was Chris Arnot, who we appointed features editor of the Telegraph after he had left Nottingham, where there was much union strife.

We became good friends and had a shared interest particularly in cricket and beer. He wrote a food/drinking column for the paper and we would often go out on lunchtime excursions to test a local hostelry.

A talented writer, Chris is now a successful author and has published many niche books. He has been a freelance journalist and author for over 25 years, writing for the *Guardian* on everything from arts and travel to education and social issues. He has also contributed to the *Observer*, *Times* and *Daily Telegraph*.

And one of the better decisions we made was on the sports desk. Roger Draper, who had joined the *Telegraph* from the *Leamington Courier*, stable mate of the *Kenilworth Weekly News*, was in charge.

I was concerned that much of his time was being spent on production processes when I felt he would be better used writing sports features and comment. He was reluctant at first but I persuaded him to give it a go.

The result was that Roger, now sadly deceased, became one of the best columnists on the *Telegrap*h. He had the ability to write biting and pertinent commentary. The only problem was that you couldn't shut him up and he over-wrote massively. However, his general impact on the sports pages was highly positive.

The heart of operations at the Telegraph in Corporation Street

In the foreground is the re-shaped news subs' table with news and sports reporters in the background. This is after Lamb's days at the Telegraph but the layout is similar and the desk from which he ejected the stand-by weather station is still in the middle of the office.

Mirrorpix

Front of house at the Telegraph

The familiar "front office" of the Corporation Street headquarters of the Coventry Evening Telegraph. There are believed to be plans to convert the area into a hotel reception and restaurant. In the heyday of the Telegraph it was frequently packed with people placing advertisements and family announcements, like births, marriages and deaths, known as the BMDs.

The inner sanctum of Lord Iliffe's flat

The boardroom on the third floor of the Corporation Street building pictured during a tour of the building by former Telegraph reporters. It overlooked the Belgrade Theatre and was part of a sumptuous suite of rooms which made up owner Lord Iliffe's flat. He was a frequent visitor and was always tended by a butler who seemed to be a permanent resident.

Exquisite walls and vintage wines

The whole of Lord Iliffe's flat was clad in this attractive and expensive-looking wooden panelling. The flat was reported to have had a very good cellar but few staff sampled the fine vintages, save for senior management. Lamb used to deliver the Times every morning to the butler, who, he imaged, carefully ironed it before presenting it to his Lordship.

Strong family foundations

The foundation stone of the Telegraph building laid by Lord (Langton) Iliffe next to the main entrance on the corner of Corporation Street and Upper Well Street on September 21, 1957. The Iliffe family also owned the Birmingham Evening Mail, Birmingham Post and Sunday Mercury among many other publications. The current Lord Iliffe (Robert, nephew of Langton) was a frequent visitor during Lamb's time at the Telegraph and this charming man was well-liked by the staff.

CHAPTER 16

Goodbye Corporation Street – finally

When permissible, I continued to do shifts on the *News of the World* in London because I wanted to keep a toehold in Fleet Street. Ann and the two young children were still in Hullbridge. I stayed with my parents in Coventry during the week and travelled home to Essex at the weekends. This allowed me to continue doing shifts on the *News of the World* when needed.

I would hop on a train from Rayleigh into Liverpool Street and then grab a Tube to St.Paul's and walk down Ludgate Hill to the *NoW* offices, housed with the *Sun* in Bouverie Street.

The *Telegraph* had been kind enough to give me a car along with the job. My son, James, then aged four, had asked who owned the car so I told him the proprietor of the *Telegraph*, Lord Iliffe, did.

Some weeks later, he was helping me wash the car (an Austin Allegro in horrible shitty brown) on the drive one Sunday morning. He poked his head above the soapy bonnet and said: "Lord Iliffe will be pleased, won't he?" I assured him he would and would tell him what a big help he had been.

Back at the *Telegraph,* we were still in the typewriter era and progress to digital technology would have been speedier but for opposition from the powerful print unions nationally.

Most of the printers on the *Telegraph* were reasonable guys and rarely caused trouble. They were our friends as well as colleagues.

I have nothing but fond memories from my last tour of the *Telegraph* in Corporation Street. One of my duties was to "train" the juniors but

I simply gathered them around and regaled them with tales about my career and Fleet Street.

During one "lesson", I showed them reports in the *Daily Mirror* and the *Daily Telegraph* of the Jeremy Thorpe trial, in which the former Liberal leader became embroiled in a political and sex scandal that ended his career.

The case arose from allegations by Norman Josiffe (otherwise known as Norman Scott) that he and Thorpe had a homosexual relationship in the early 1960s, and that Thorpe had begun a badly-planned conspiracy to murder Josiffe, who was threatening to expose their affair. All defendants were eventually acquitted.

On this day, the *Daily Telegraph* ran a two-page report of the previous day's hearing at the Old Bailey. It was really an exercise in shorthand and typing. The *Mirror* report, though, was only about 20 paragraphs long but I held it up as a perfect example of skilled journalism.

Through clever reporting and sub-editing there wasn't a redundant word in the report and you did not feel you had missed anything in comparison with the *Daily Telegraph* version.

Most of my "trainees" were ambitious to reach Fleet Street and many of them did. Andrew Grice and David Brindle went into newspapers and forged distinguished careers in the national media.

Roger Harrabin, brother of Brian, whose firm won the contract to convert the *Telegraph* building into a hotel, and David Shukman, one of the nicest guys I ever met in journalism, went on to join the BBC and still report regularly.

Crime reporter Annette Witheridge did gruelling shifts as a freelance in London and then landed staff jobs on the *Star* and the *News of the World*. She eventually created her own news agency in New York and thrived there for over 20 years before returning permanently to the UK in 2019.

Sarah Compton had a hugely successful career in Fleet Street and was the *Daily Telegraph*'s arts editor for many years. And Rachel Campey was to become editor of the *Evening Herald* in Plymouth, the *Express & Echo* in Exeter and the *Yorkshire Post*.

In fact the *Telegraph* became a maturing ground for many women who pioneered female journalism at a time when their presence was still frowned upon in some quarters. Few concessions were made to their sex and they would not have had it any other way.

With my training hat on, I recounted a story that still holds good to this day. Working practices and attitudes began to change at the *Telegraph*. When Geoff fell ill for some weeks, I found myself in the editor's chair in the very same office that I had discovered the chief reporter grovelling on the floor all of those years before.

The office was on the corner overlooking Corporation Street but the layout of the furniture had been changed and I'm sure the carpet would have been different.

We used to take conference in there every morning to discuss the shape of that day's paper. On one day there was a trial in Coventry of a youngster accused of murder where identification was an issue because of the age of some witnesses.

The accused clearly liked harming children and we felt he should be exposed. Later that morning I received call from my old friend Keith Whetstone, then editor-in-chief of *The Post and Mail* in Birmingham, saying he was going to ask the judge if the names could be reported and asked me to be a signatory to the request.

I said I wouldn't because I felt it was a risk we should take on our own and not seek official sanction. But he went ahead anyway and later told me the judge had said he felt naming the accused would not be illegal but "manifestly unfair".

Like Keith, I had taken legal advice which said we would be safe to report the names with any comeback unlikely.

Keith's advice, he told me, had been the opposite. Anyway, we went ahead and published. Nothing happened except that the identity of a very sinister and perverted young person was exposed.

Geoff was an excellent leader writer and even won prizes for his skills. Me not so. But I remember writing one about two Coventry City players who got into trouble with the club after going out on the razzle on the eve of a match.

At the time, the country was going through a severe recession with unemployment soaring. I suggested in the opinion column of the paper on Saturday, January 2, 1982, that the actions of the footballers were unacceptable when most ordinary people were going through extreme austerity.

I was pleased with my leader column, and especially the headline: "A question of support", an allusion to *A Question of Sport* on BBC television.

I had a small office between the space outside Geoff's and the feature writers, who now occupied the old reporters' room I remembered from my copy boy days.

Feature writers, probably unjustly, were always regarded as the luvvies of newspapers and one day a delegation squeezed into my office to complain that they were not being given enough "thinking time" to write their wonderful prose.

I had a quick think about it and told them in the nicest possible way to fuck off and get on with it.

I also had a desk on the editorial floor. When I first occupied it I found a load of metal and plastic junk held together by string in the bottom right-hand drawer. I promptly dumped it into the wastebasket.

"Crossie" was apoplectic when he discovered what I had done. This was apparently the standby weather station for the one of the roof.

To save money, "Crossie" had engaged a local school to do the weather forecast for us and they used to visit the roof every day to read contraptions built, I imagine, by the ever-resourceful deputy editor.

It was while sitting at that desk that I received a phone call from Dave Shapland, who was deputy sports editor when I worked on the *News of the World*. He had been made deputy editor on the *Sun* by editor Kelvin MacKenzie.

Dave told me that he wanted me to become assistant night editor on the *Sun*. It came as a shock and I explained that I was very happy at the *Telegraph*.

However, he gave me some time to think about it and got back to him next day and told him thanks but no thanks. The next day, Kelvin was on the phone. I explained that I had a contract with three months notice on the *Telegraph* and that I didn't want to upset them by leaving so early.

"I'll send a DR up for your contract," said Kelvin, "and our lawyers will blow holes through it". The DR did, indeed, turn up in a few hours but I sent him away empty handed.

As mentioned, these were times of severe austerity and my salary on the *Telegraph* was fairly meagre but better than some. It was around £13,000 a year as I remember and when Kelvin came back on, saying they would up the salary to £21,000 plus expenses, I gave in.

I think Geoff was genuinely sad to see me go. The lure of Fleet Street was too great for me and I departed on very amicable terms.

So I headed off south again to enjoy my first weeks in the Waldorf Hotel near Covent Garden between Fleet Street and the Strand courtesy of the *Sun*.

My hours were horrendous – 3pm to 3am. On my first day – a Sunday – I marched off to Kelvin's office for him to introduce me to my new colleagues, who knew nothing of my appointment.

But that's another story...

Back to London after an offer from the Sun that was too tempting to turn down.

Registered Office:
News Group Newspapers Ltd.
A Subsidiary of News International Ltd.
30 Bouverie Street, Fleet Street, London, EC4Y 8DE.

Registered No. 679215 England
Telex: Sunnews 267827
Telephone 01-353 3030

Letter of Appointment

It is agreed that Mr. John Lamb will join The Sun as Assistant Night Editor at a salary of £21,000 per annum.

The above salary includes an amount for covenanted overtime as agreed between the management and the NUJ chapel.

Under this agreement Mr. Lamb will be expected to work extra time on each shift as laid down by his department head.

Holidays and other arrangements are as stated in the house agreement between the NUJ and this company.

The period of notice will be three months on either side.

The signature of both parties on this document is binding.

Richard M. Parrack
Editorial Manager

John Lamb

18th May, 1982

Back on their old stomping ground

Former Coventry Evening Telegraph reporters who made it big in London (left to right): David Brindle, Roger Harrabin and Andy Grice. They are pictured in the Telegraph's original newsroom overlooking Belgrade Square during a tour of the then-deserted building after the Telegraph moved to its current offices. The visit for former journalists was arranged by Roger's brother, Brian, whose company is handling the redevelopment of the building into a hotel and student accommodation.

Charlie Porter in his glory...

John Lamb wrote a tribute in the Coventry Evening Telegraph when his old boss, the eccentric Charles E Porter, retired as editor of the Kenilworth Weekly News (KWN) in 1977.

This is a cutting of part of the feature. The picture shows Charlie in his element, touring along Kenilworth High Street with his bike. Everyone knew him even though he never used his own name in the paper.

When he wrote a critique of a play at the Talisman or Priory theatres, he would do so under the pseudonym Tutivillus, who was said in Christian folklore to be a demon associated with writing and literacy.

Charlie must have chosen the moniker with tongue in cheek. The KWN was famous, if not infamous, for its silly headlines largely penned by Charlie. People were known to buy the paper just to check out his latest creations, which Lamb highlights in the chapter called Silly headlines and a lady's bike.

He headlined a feature about a rabbit fancier 'He Keeps Furries at the Bottom of his Garden', the report of an accident in which a driver broke his nose 'Car in Ditch, Broken Snitch' . . .

Chas Porter with his method of transport o "Weekly News" offices i Road, Kenilwort

Vintage Porter

JOHN LAMB

on a newspaperman with a highly individual style.

THIS article would probably have been placed firmly on Chas. E. Porter's spike.

As the editor of one of Warwickshire's smallest newspapers, he has a style all of his own. And the way this story is written is not the way of Chas. E. Porter.

He retires this month after near 28 years in the chair of the Kenilworth's Weekly News," virtually a one-man operation until about 16 years ago when I joined him as his first "junior."

Now the Porter era comes to an end — and with it one of the most individual and eccentric newspapers in the country is likely to make more conventional reading.

For no-one could imitate the style of Chas. Porter.

When I arrived at the offices of the "Comic," Mr Porter's nickname for the "Weekly News," it was in the fondly-held belief that newspapers offered something of a glamorous occupation.

This foolishness soon faded when I was issued with the office transport — a lady's bike.

From then on, the whole world of newspapers took on a different meaning.

In those days the editor and I lived in Coventry. Editorial conferences took place about 200 yards from the junction of the A45 on the Kenilworth Road.

A roadside ditch became the office as we exchanged "copy" and I was sent on my way to the printers in Leamington by Midland Red bus while the editor left in the other direction

port involving a car hitting a wall, witnessed by a window cleaner) were others I recall.

But the classic was "Bear Virgins and Lion in Spicey Finale."

An exciting headline for something utterly mundane — a report of a

The "Weekly News" of grand affair in Kenilwo street, used to be a two-r tucked away from the t But Chas. Porter was r found there.

At nearly 65, he is s astride his bicycle (he correspondent for the Evening Telegraph") ex lanes of Kenilworth spor shorts and a day's growth

His distate for pompo was reflected in the wa nearly always arrive for " do's" by bicycle, and "for off his bike-clips before scene of a grand gatheri

His influence on civi Kenilworth may not be parent, but he is o journalists actually to l buted to council debate from the Press table to m

Chas. Porter is also a the fact that he is prob of that rare breed handling almost every newspaper production.

The Author

John Lamb

John Lamb was born in Kenilworth. His family – mum Maud, dad George and brother Colin – had been evacuated when their home in Cheveral Avenue, Coventry, near the then Daimler factory, was destroyed by Hitler's bombing blitz.

The family returned to the house after war-time reparations and John grew up on the streets of Radford (well, in his parents' house too).

His school experience at Barkers Butts was totally undistinguished and when he left at 15 he did not have a qualification to his name.

Save for, that is, a diploma from the Boy Scouts for swimming a length at breast stroke and four London College of Music (they became royal later) certificates for piano playing and music theory.

The young Lamb was going to become an electrician but he was introduced to the world of newspapers by pure chance and helped the *Coventry Evening Telegraph* move into their new offices and printing works in Corporation Street in 1960.

He joined the *Telegraph* as a copy (office) boy and after several disappointments eventually worked as a journalist on the weekly paper in Kenilworth and major evenings in the Midlands and Fleet Street.

On the way he gained an elusive qualification that he craved – the National Council for the Training of Journalists Proficiency Certificate – to prove that he was not as thick as plaster, as he feared.

His daughter Joanne now runs her own hairdressing business and son James is a head teacher in Somerset.

John still works – as director of press and PR at Greater Birmingham Chambers of Commerce, producing a large monthly business magazine, a daily news bulletin, weekly newsletters, podcasts, blogs and much comment in the media. He appears frequently on television and radio.

He has resumed playing the piano and is in a group called Second Chance, along with one his of his current work colleagues, Phil Parkin.

He also pursues a lasting interest in classical music and jazz while still enjoying regular pints at the Royal Oak in Earlsdon, Coventry.

John is a former chairman of Birmingham Press Club and is currently vice-president with ITV's veteran newscaster Bob Warman as president.

- *John Lamb's views in Telegraph People are not necessarily those of Greater Birmingham Chambers of Commerce, where he is director of Press and PR.*

Footnote by John Lamb

Bob Cole, former photographer on the Coventry Evening Telegraph, was a great help to me in researching pictures for Telegraph People. Sadly, Bob has passed away.

A larger-than-life character, he was first and foremost a great photographer but was always prepared to have a laugh at his own expense.

He often recalled the time when he went out on a job with his camera but not a film in those pre-digital times. This resulted in a sign being put over the photographers' room exit stating: BOB - DON'T FORGET A FILM!

Another lapse of memory on Bob's part resulted in the sign being changed to: BOB - DON'T FORGET YOUR CAMERA!

He will be sadly missed but fond memories will linger.

Bob with daughter Karena

Out in Autumn 2020

Late night FINAL

By John Lamb

This semi-biographical account of a different age in newspapers and Britain traces the life and career of a journalist who experiences bridge 60 years from hot metal production to the digital revolution.

Lamb recounts the final days of flourishing London, Birmingham and Coventry regional evening newspapers when they produced multiple editions every day, carrying breaking news in the only printed source available.

Newspapers featured include the *London Evening News, London Standard, Birmingham Evening Mail,* and *Coventry Evening Telegraph,* the daily *Birmingham Post* and the tiny *Kenilworth Weekly News* along with stories from inside the Fleet Street offices of the *Sun*, the *News of the World* and the *Daily Mirror* in the Eighties.